A PRACTICAL GUIDE

TO EVALUATING DECKS

A PRACTICAL GUIDE

TO EVALUATING DECKS

Bruce A. Barker

A Practical Guide to Evaluating Decks

Copyright © 2021 by Dream Home Consultants, LLC. All rights reserved. No part of this book may be reproduced or retransmitted in any form or by any means without the written permission of the copyright holder.

Revised July 2021

Publisher's Cataloging-in-Publication Data

Bruce A. Barker

A practical guide to evaluating decks / Bruce A. Barker

Includes bibliographic references.

ISBN 13: 978-0-9848160-6-4

1. Housing- Standards --Popular works. 2. Building laws--Popular works.   3. Dwellings--Design and construction--Standards--Popular works. I Title.

Disclaimer of Liability

Every effort has been made to ensure the accuracy of the material contained in this book. The author, Dream Home Consultants, LLC., and printer assume no liability whatsoever for any loss or damages caused by the use of or interpretation of the material in this book. The author, Dream Home Consultants, LLC, and printer disclaim liability to any and all parties for any and all losses or damages including, but not limited to, incidental and consequential damages and losses or damages caused by deficiencies, errors, or omissions contained in this book regardless of whether such deficiencies, errors, or omissions result from negligence or any other cause or theory. The author, Dream Home Consultants, LLC, and printer recommend that the reader consult the local building official and qualified professionals before and during all projects.

ACKNOWLEDGMENTS

COPY EDITING

Ashley Kairis

ILLUSTRATIONS

Bruce A. Barker

PHOTOGRAPHS

Bruce A. Barker

Patrick Berger

John Cauthen

John Cranor

Joseph Loferski

JT McConnell

Randy Sipe

Dutton Smith

Jerrod Turnbow

Frank Woeste

REFERENCES

American Heritage Dictionary of the English Language
Fifth Edition

Design for Code Acceptance 6 (DCA 6-2015)
American Wood Council

Dictionary of Architecture and Construction, Fourth Edition
Cyril M. Harris

Garner's Modern American Usage, Second Edition
Bryan A. Garner

International Residential Code 2018
International Code Council, Inc

The Chicago Manual of Style, 15th Edition

TABLE OF CONTENTS

1 - INTRODUCTION TO DECK EVALUATION 1

2 - DECK FLASHING 21

3 - DECK ATTACHMENT TO THE BUILDING 31

4 - GUARDS AND HANDRAILS 53

5 - STAIRWAYS AND LANDINGS 79

6 - DECK FRAMING 103

7 - DECK POSTS AND FOOTINGS 133

8 - DECK ELECTRICAL REQUIREMENTS 147

APPENDIXES

A - DECK EVALUATION PROTOCOL 151

B - ASHI DECK INSPECTION STANDARD
     OF PRACTICE 153

C - DECK EVALUATION CHECKLIST 161

D - DECK FAILURES 169

E - GLOSSARY 183

F - RESOURCES 191

DETAILED TABLE OF CONTENTS

1 - INTRODUCTION TO DECK EVALUATION 1
- IS YOUR DECK SAFE? 1
- LOOKS AREN'T EVERYTHING 2
- OBJECTIVE AND SCOPE OF THIS BOOK 6
- DEFINITION OF A DECK 7
- STANDARD OF PRACTICE 9
- HOW TO USE THIS BOOK 9
- WHAT IS THE GOAL WHEN EVALUATING A DECK? 11
- BUILDING CODES 101 11
- WHEN WAS THAT REQUIREMENT ADDED? 13
- WHAT IS UNSAFE? 13
- BUILDING CODES VERSUS BEST PRACTICES 15
- LOCAL BUILDING CODES VERSUS BEST PRACTICES 15
- FOR HOMEOWNERS 16
  - Construction of Older Decks 16
  - Decks Built During New Construction 17
  - Decks Added or Replaced 18
- SAFETY FIRST – A CASE STUDY 19

2 - DECK FLASHING 21
- OVERVIEW 21
- IMPLICATIONS OF DECK FLASHING FAILURE 21
- GENERAL DECK FLASHING REQUIREMENTS 22
- HISTORY 25
- 2.1 - DEFECT – ABSENT, IMPROPERLY INSTALLED, DAMAGED, AND DETERIORATED DECK FLASHING 25

3 - DECK ATTACHMENT TO THE BUILDING 31

OVERVIEW 31
IMPLICATIONS OF DECK LEDGER BOARD DETACHMENT 33
GENERAL DECK LEDGER BOARD ATTACHMENT REQUIREMENTS 33
HISTORY 36
3.1 - DEFECT – NAILED OR SCREWED DECK LEDGER BOARD 37
3.2 - DEFECT – DECK LEDGER BOARD ATTACHED
THROUGH WALL COVERINGS 38
3.3 - DEFECT – IMPROPER DECK LEDGER BOARD
FASTENER TYPE OR QUANTITY 40
3.4 - DEFECT – IMPROPER DECK LEDGER BOARD
FASTENER SPACING AND LOCATION 41
3.5 - DEFECT – BUILDING BAND JOIST OR RIM BOARD
DOES NOT BEAR ON THE FOUNDATION 42
3.6 - DEFECT – DECK LEDGER BOARD NOT ATTACHED
TO AN APPROVED COMPONENT 45
3.7 - DEFECT – LATERAL LOAD CONNECTORS NOT INSTALLED 48
3.8 - DEFECT – DETERIORATED OR DAMAGED WOOD 48
3.9 - DEFECT – DETERIORATED HARDWARE 50

4 - GUARDS AND HANDRAILS 53

OVERVIEW 53
IMPLICATIONS OF GUARD AND HANDRAIL FAILURE 53
GENERAL GUARD AND HANDRAIL REQUIREMENTS 53
HISTORY 57
4.1 - DEFECT – GUARD POST INSTALLATION DEFECTS 58
4.2 - DEFECT – GUARD INSTALLATION DEFECTS 66
4.3 - DEFECT – GUARD FILL-IN COMPONENT
INSTALLATION DEFECTS 67
4.4 - DEFECT – HANDRAIL INSTALLATION DEFECTS 72
4.5 - DEFECT – DECK COMPONENTS PENETRATE
WALL COVERINGS 75

4.6 - DEFECT – DETERIORATED, DAMAGED, AND
LOOSE GUARDS, HANDRAILS, AND HARDWARE 76

5 - STAIRWAYS AND LANDINGS 79

OVERVIEW 79
IMPLICATIONS OF DECK STAIRWAY FAILURE 79
GENERAL STAIRWAY AND LANDING REQUIREMENTS 80
HISTORY 83

5.1 - DEFECT – IMPROPER RISER HEIGHT, TREAD DEPTH,
AND NOSING DEPTH 84

5.2 - DEFECT – IMPROPER RISER HEIGHT, TREAD DEPTH,
AND NOSING DEPTH DIFFERENCES 85

5.3 - DEFECT – RISER OPENING BETWEEN TREADS
ALLOWS 4-INCH DIAMETER SPHERE TO PASS 86

5.4 - DEFECT – INADEQUATE STRINGER SUPPORT AT
DECK OR TOP OF LANDING 87

5.5 - DEFECT – IMPROPER DROP HEADER INSTALLATION 91

5.6 - DEFECT – IMPROPER STRINGER SUPPORT AT THE
BOTTOM OF THE STAIRWAY 93

5.7 - DEFECT – STRINGER INSTALLATION DEFECTS 95

5.8 - DEFECT – IMPROPER STRINGER INTERMEDIATE SUPPORT 97

5.9 - DEFECT – TREAD INSTALLATION DEFECTS 98

5.10 - DEFECT – LANDING DEFECTS 100

5.11 - DEFECT – DETERIORATED AND DAMAGED
STAIRWAYS AND HARDWARE 101

6 - DECK FRAMING 103

OVERVIEW 103
IMPLICATIONS OF DECK FRAMING FAILURE 103
GENERAL DECK FRAMING REQUIREMENTS 103
HISTORY 108
6.1 - DEFECT – DECK FLOOR JOISTS OR BEAMS OVER-SPANNED ... 109

6.2 - DEFECT – DECK FLOOR JOISTS SUPPORTED BY FASTENERS, ANGLE BRACKET, OR LEDGER STRIP 111

6.3 - DEFECT – DECK FLOOR JOISTS OR BEAMS EXCESSIVELY NOTCHED OR BORED 114

6.4 - DEFECT – IMPROPER JOIST HANGER AND CONNECTOR INSTALLATION 116

6.5 - DEFECT – CANTILEVERED DECK FLOOR JOISTS NOT BLOCKED AT DECK BEAM 120

6.6 - DEFECT – DECK BEAM MEMBERS NOT ADEQUATELY FASTENED TO EACH OTHER 121

6.7 - DEFECT – IMPROPER DECK BEAM ATTACHMENT TO THE DECK LEDGER BOARD 121

6.8 - DEFECT – DECK BEAM ATTACHED TO SIDE OF DECK POST 122

6.9 - DEFECT – DECK BEAM NOT PROPERLY SECURED TO DECK POST 124

6.10 - DEFECT – DECK BEAM NOT SUPPORTED BY DECK POST 125

6.11 - DEFECT – SPLICE IN MULTIPLE-MEMBER DECK BEAM IS NOT SUPPORTED BY A DECK POST 127

6.12 - DEFECT – DECK BRACING DEFECTS 128

6.13 - DEFECT – DECK FLOORING DEFECTS 129

6.14 - DEFECT – DETERIORATED AND DAMAGED DECK FRAMING AND HARDWARE 130

7 - DECK POSTS AND FOOTINGS 133

OVERVIEW 133

IMPLICATIONS OF DECK POST AND FOOTING FAILURE 133

GENERAL DECK POST AND FOOTING REQUIREMENTS 133

HISTORY 135

7.1 - DEFECT – DECK POST TOO TALL 136

7.2 - DEFECT – DECK POST NATURAL DEFECTS 136

7.3 - DEFECT – DECK POST NOT PLUMB 138

7.4 - DEFECT – DECK POST NOT IN CENTER OF FOOTING 139

7.5 - DEFECT – DECK POST NOT SECURED AT THE BOTTOM OF THE POST 140

7.6 - DEFECT – DECK FOOTING TOO SMALL OR DAMAGED 141

7.7 - DEFECT – DECK FOOTING WITHIN FIVE FEET FROM THE BUILDING FOUNDATION 143

7.8 - DEFECT – DETERIORATED AND DAMAGED DECK POSTS AND HARDWARE 144

8 - DECK ELECTRICAL REQUIREMENTS 147

OVERVIEW 147

IMPLICATIONS OF DECK ELECTRICAL REQUIREMENTS FAILURE ... 147

GENERAL DECK ELECTRICAL REQUIREMENTS 147

HISTORY 148

8.1 - DEFECT – ABSENT DECK-RELATED LIGHTING 148

8.2 - DEFECT – ABSENT DECK-RELATED RECEPTACLE 148

8.3 - DEFECT – INADEQUATE CLEARANCE TO OVERHEAD ELECTRICAL WIRES 149

APPENDIXES

A - DECK EVALUATION PROTOCOL 151

B - ASHI DECK INSPECTION STANDARD OF PRACTICE 153

C - DECK EVALUATION CHECKLIST 161

D - DECK FAILURES 169

E - GLOSSARY 183

F - RESOURCES 191

PREFACE

Real estate agents who work with me joke that I never met a deck that I liked. Fair enough. But, having been a home inspector for more than twenty years, I know what safe deck looks like, and I know that **few decks are as safe as they should be.**

Often I would come home after inspections and show my wife pictures of unsafe decks. She was surprised that so many were unsafe, and she urged me to start writing about deck safety.

My first book about decks became *Deck Codes and Standards* (published by Black + Decker). It is held by most public libraries in the country, and is also available elsewhere.

While I was writing *Deck Codes and Standards* my focus was the problems that I had seen. My wife, however, started looking into the research. This led her to Dr. Joe Loferski and Dr. Frank Woeste, both at Virginia Tech, and later to Dr. Don Bender at Washington State.

After seeing the latest research, and learning that the prescriptive standard was DCA6, I incorporated much of that information into the book. In addition, we met with Dr. Woeste, and learned that for many years he had been compiling a list of the deck failures reported in the news. Working with him, we updated the list (Appendix D: Deck Failures). Although the information in this appendix is disressing, we felt, as he did, that it was an important aid in helping the public understand that deck safety is a very serious issue.

So, that is the backstory. Now, what is this book about?

When people think about their deck, they usually think in terms of how it looks from the top. If the part of the deck that they see and that they walk on looks good, then they believe that the deck is in good shape. Few go under the deck to look at the important structural components, and few would know what they were looking at even if they did. This is one reason why each year there are injuries and fatalities when an unsafe deck fails.

Another reason is that people believe that a deck is safe if it passed a code inspection. This is not always true, for reasons that I explain in Chapter 1. For now, know that the important question is: "Is the deck safe today?" It does not matter whether the deck passed code inspection today, or years ago. What matters is the condition of the deck when you, your family, or your friends walk on it.

This book is not intended for people who want to build a deck. There are plenty of books on that subject.

This book is intended for people who want to evaluate the condition of an existing deck, and for people who want to find examples of mistakes to avoid. We believe that deck-related injuries and fatalities are avoidable if people take a few relatively inexpensive steps to make sure that their decks are built and maintained with safety in mind.

As far as we know, this is the only book of its kind. We have tried to make this book accessible both to building inspection professionals and to homeowners. **The deck inspection checklist in Appendix C is supported by over 150 pictures and illustrations. The checklist, pictures, and illustrations should help readers identify most of the defects that are likely to cause a deck failure.**

Although this book is intended for everyone who is interested in deck safety, a few words of caution are appropriate. Decks are more complicated than most people realize. Homeowners who evaluate their own decks using this book should defer to a building inspection professional if there are any questions about how to apply the material in this book. Building inspection professionals should defer to a qualified specialist, such as a structural engineer, when an issue is beyond the scope of their knowledge, skill, and experience. This is especially true when recommending what to do about an issue.

Finally, be careful when you go under a deck, and when you walk on deck stairs. While it is uncommon, an unsafe deck can collapse just from people walking on it. A deck or a stairway can collapse when people are working under it, or even while they are just inspecting it. Look at the condition of the deck and of the stairway before you go under the deck or use the stairs.

Avoid going under a deck if it appears to be older or in poor condition. Avoid using the stairs if they appear to be unstable, or if they appear to be in poor condition. If you suspect that the deck is in poor condition, do not attempt to evaluate the deck on your own. Someone with technical expertise should be there to help with a preliminary examination, and to help you determine if there is a problem.

As I hope you have realized, we want readers to find this book a valuable resource for improving deck safety. Toward that end, the following page summarizes the main points that readers should consider.

SUMMARY

The front matter (the material before the first chapter) might seem an odd place to find a summary of this book. The reason for this summary is the pre-training principle. It states that people learn better if they know the basic concepts before being exposed to the details. Below are some of the important concepts presented in this book.

- Is the deck safe today? Whether or not the deck was code-compliant or safe in the past does not matter.
- Building codes are a minimum standard. They are not intended to present best practices.
- Model building codes are slow to adopt best practices. Model building codes had almost no guidance about deck construction until about 2009. While guidance improved in each edition from 2009 to 2018, model building codes do not present best practices.
- Governments are slow to adopt the most current model building code. A deck built using the most current <u>local</u> building code could be built under a building code that is many years out-of-date.
- Passing inspection does not mean that the deck is code-compliant or safe. Building officials are not responsible for ensuring code-compliance. The deck builder is responsible for code compliance and for safety.
- Manufacturer's instructions rule. Read and follow manufacturer's instructions when installing deck components.
- Proper flashing where the deck attaches to the house is essential. It does not matter how many bolts or screws you install in rotten wood, the bolts or screws will not secure the deck to the house as intended.
- Deck failures often occur because the deck ledger detaches from the house. Proper attachment of the deck ledger to the house is essential for safety.
- Injuries often occur because the deck guard detaches from the deck. Safe attachment of guard posts to the deck requires more than just bolts that are attached to deck rim joists.
- Improper stairway construction is a common cause of deck-related injuries. Proper construction of deck stairways, guards, and handrails is essential for safety.

1: INTRODUCTION TO DECK EVALUATION

IS YOUR DECK SAFE?

We have not found reliable information about the actual number of deck-related injuries and fatalities, and it is not for lack of effort. Based on news reports that we have found, and based on inspections of hundreds of decks, **the actual number of deck-related injuries and fatalities is high enough to make deck safety a concern for everyone who walks on a deck.**

Please refer to Appendix D to see a list of reported deck-related injuries and fatalities between 2001 and 2020. This list almost certainly under-represents deck-related injuries because many such injuries are not reported in the news.

Even without reliable numbers, it is fair to say that:

- **even newer decks that were built with a permit and with inspections may not be as safe as they should be.** This is due, in part, to differences in adoption and enforcement of building codes among building departments, and due to the fact that building codes are slow to adopt deck construction best practices. Refer to Building Codes 101 in this chapter for more about the limitations of building codes and government inspections.
- **the possibility of deck-related injuries and deaths increases for older decks.** One reason is that before 2009 there was a lack of detail in building codes about how to build a deck. Another reason is that deck materials deteriorate when exposed to the weather. The graph on the following page is a visual representation of the increasing risks of older decks.

2   1: Introduction to Deck Evaluation

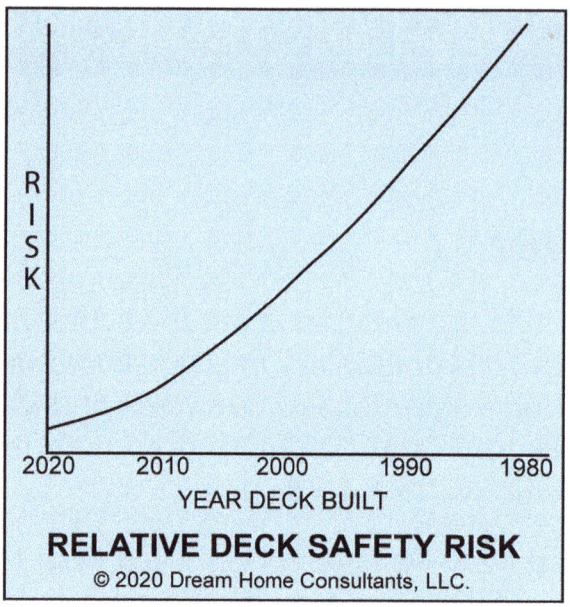

Figure 1

LOOKS AREN'T EVERYTHING

Please do not let anyone convince you that pressure washing and a fresh coat of stain will "restore" the deck. These actions may restore the **appearance** of the deck, for a while, but cleaning and staining will not restore the structural safety of the deck. Structural safety matters; looks, not so much.

You must evaluate the entire deck, not just the parts that you can easily see, in order to find out what you really need to do in order to restore the deck. You may be able to make improvements that at least partially restore the deck. Only then should you think about pressure washing and staining the deck. If the deck is older, however, you should be prepared for the possibility that it may be more cost-effective to replace it.

Here are a few examples of defects that you might find when you evaluate the entire deck. These defects might not cause a deck failure for years, or they might cause a deck failure during your next party, or even when nobody is present.

Figure 2

This deteriorated house rim joist illustrates why deck flashing is important. The deck ledger that was attached to this deteriorated house rim joist may have caused the deck to collapse no matter how many bolts were installed.

Figure 3

Improper deck ledger attachment. Look closely at the small screws that were used to attach this deck ledger through siding. This deck could collapse during your next party.

Figure 4

Posts in the ground are allowed, but are not recommended. Buried posts may look solid from the outside, but when you probe just below the soil, you may find that they are almost hollow. This is caused by constant exposure to moisture. Do not let people on a deck that is supported by deteriorated posts.

Figure 5

Even preservative-treated wood and galvanized hardware deteriorate. This picture is an example of obvious deterioration, but even much less obvious deterioration can reduce the strength of wood and metal.

Figure 6

This is an example of what may happen if deck stairs are not properly supported. Would you want to walk on these stairs?

Figure 7

Notched guard posts are not allowed because the post can split at the notch and the guard can collapse if someone leans on the guard. Also note the new-looking wood on an old deck. Attaching new wood to an old deck seldom does much good, and may give a false sense of security.

OBJECTIVE AND SCOPE OF THIS BOOK

So, how do you evaluate a deck? This book provides a practical guide and a checklist to help you through the evaluation process, regardless of the age of the deck. Decks that may be evaluated using this guide and checklist are those that:

- are made primarily using preservative-treated wood or naturally durable wood, including those using typical alternative materials such as composites, metal, and plastic;
- have one flat horizontal surface (a single level deck);
- are at least as wide as they are long;
- have posts that are not more than 14 feet tall;
- are associated with buildings that are classified as one-family or two-family dwellings;

- have components that are mostly visible for evaluation;
- are not located in seismic, high wind, or very heavy snow design areas, and;
- do not support loads such as roofs, and do not support concentrated loads such as spas and hot tubs.

People may wish to use this guide and checklist to evaluate other decks. Using the information in this book to evaluate out-of-scope decks may require additional resources and expertise in order to address situations and defects not covered in this book.

DEFINITION OF A DECK

For purposes of this book, a deck is a horizontal wood-framed structure that is located outside of the building, and that is supported by posts or similar structural components at two or more locations. A deck may be called a balcony, landing, stairway, or porch. A deck may be attached to the building, or it may be freestanding.

For purposes of this book, structures that are not considered to be a deck include cantilevered structures such as balconies and stairway landings, structures supported entirely on grade, and structures supported on continuous footings.

Figure 8

Beware when evaluating cantilevered structures.

8 1: Introduction to Deck Evaluation

A deck is an interconnected system consisting of many components. In many cases, the components work together. Each component must function properly for the deck system to perform safely over the service life of the deck. Understanding that a deck is an interconnected system is important when evaluating a deck. Refer to Figures 9 and 10.

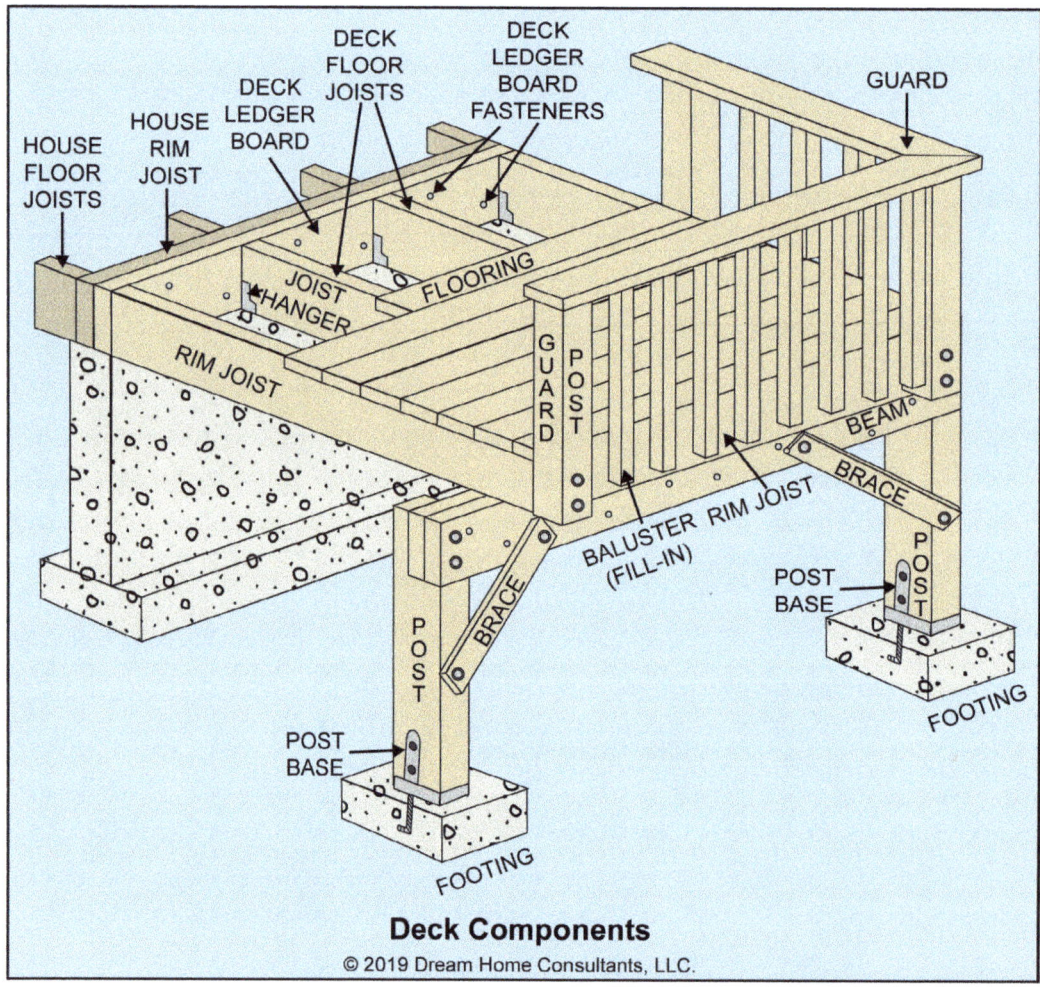

Figure 9

1: Introduction to Deck Evaluation

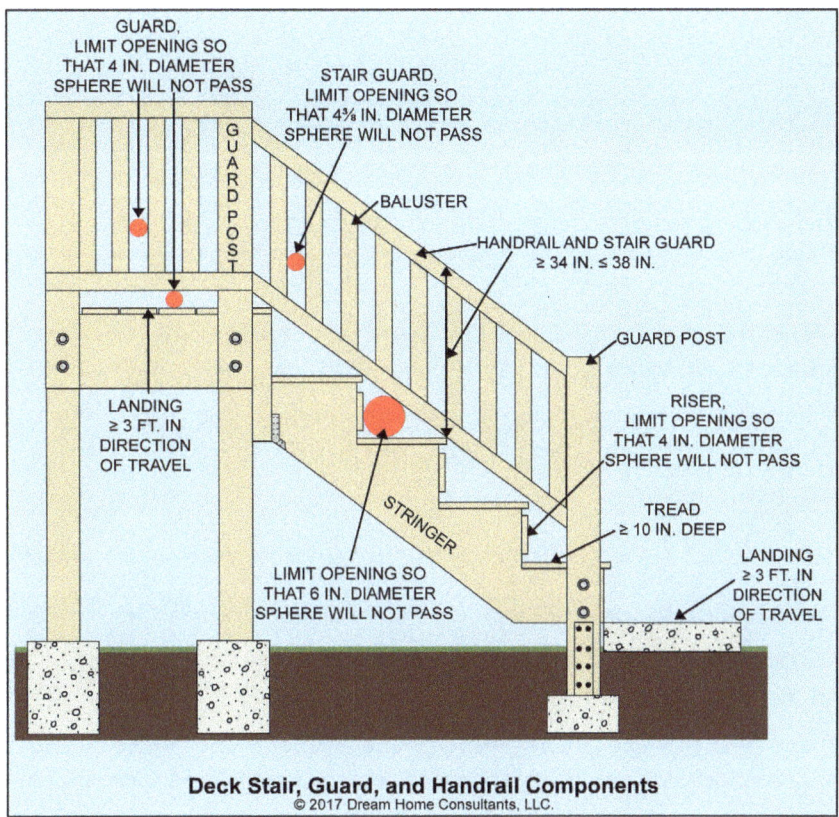

Figure 10

STANDARD OF PRACTICE

A Standard of Practice (SOP) should be used when evaluating a deck, especially when doing so for compensation. This book uses the American Society of Home Inspectors Auxiliary Standard of Professional Practice for Residential Deck Inspections (ASHI Deck SOP) as the guideline for determining deck components that should be evaluated. Refer to the ASHI Deck SOP in Appendix B.

HOW TO USE THIS BOOK

This book provides an integrated approach to evaluating a deck. You will find the deck evaluation checklist in Appendix C. The checklist references information in this book in order to help people identify and evaluate most common deck defects. Note that it is not practical to list all defects, so the checklist does not include less-common defects.

The checklist references a discussion about each major deck component category. For example, we discuss deck flashing in the next chapter of this book. Each discussion contains several parts, including:

- an overview of the deck component that explains what the component does, and why the component is important;
- an explanation of the implications if the deck component fails;
- an explanation of the current general requirements for installing the deck component, along with illustrations showing the current installation recommendations (This general requirements explanation is not intended to be an in-depth explanation of all current deck construction recommendations.);
- a brief history of how the deck component installation requirements have changed over time.

The checklist also references common defects encountered when evaluating a deck. For example, absent or improperly installed deck flashing is Defect Number 2.1 in Chapter 2, Deck Flashing. Most defect discussions contain a description of:

- the defect, often with one or more pictures of what the defect may look like;
- why the defect might cause a deck failure;
- the safety risk created by the defect, and why the condition may be unsafe;
- what the deck evaluator might consider recommending about what someone should do to address the defect; and
- a possible way to repair the defect.

The checklist includes a column for recording the condition of the component. There is also a column for recording whether there is a recommendation that the component should be evaluated by a specialist (such as an engineer), or whether the deck owner should take action to address the defect. Refer to the suggested Deck Evaluation Protocol (Appendix A) in this book for descriptions of the entries in the checklist columns.

WHAT IS THE GOAL WHEN EVALUATING A DECK?

When evaluating a deck, the first question you should ask: "**Is the deck safe?**" You might also want to know if the deck complied with the building code when it was built, and when a particular deck construction feature was required.

Determining if a new deck complies with current building code is difficult enough because building codes are subject to interpretation. **Determining if an old deck complied with the building code when the deck was built is almost impossible.** Besides, building code compliance is often relevant only to the building official who is evaluating a new deck, the real estate agent or home seller who is determining who should pay for a deck issue raised by a home inspector, and the attorney who is building a case involving losses incurred because of a deck failure. For the rest of us, the third goal is more relevant. After all, **safety should be the primary goal.**

Though, one may ask: "Isn't a code-compliant deck safe to use?" The answer is, it depends. **A code-compliant deck may, or may not, have been safe to use when it was built.** The current condition of the deck, however, depends on many factors, for example: the age of the deck, the environment in which the deck exists, the materials and methods used to build the deck, and the maintenance of the deck, just to name a few.

Evaluating a deck, therefore, involves more than determining code compliance. In fact, determining code compliance is so difficult, and in many circumstances irrelevant, especially for an older deck. It is more productive to focus on other factors when evaluating a deck.

BUILDING CODES 101

Building codes and building officials play a very important part in deck safety, but they are not the only part, and they have limitations. In order to better understand these limitations, it helps to understand more about building codes, and more about the code enforcement process.

- **It is possible that a deck that is approved by a building official is, in fact, not building code compliant.** Building officials are not responsible for ensuring building code compliance. Their job is to use their best efforts to determine building code-compliance. The person pulling the building permit is responsible for ensuring building code compliance.

- **Building codes are a minimum standard.** They are not intended to be best practices. A deck built according to best practices is more likely to be safe compared to one built according to a minimum building code.

- **There is no national building code (in the United States).** Building codes issued by organizations, such as the International Code Council (ICC) and the National Fire Protection Association (NFPA), are model (recommended) codes. These codes have no legal effect until they are adopted by a state or a local government. This being the case, it is not possible to determine code-compliance without drilling down to the state and the local level.

- **State and local governments usually change the model building codes when they adopt them.** These changes can significantly change the model building code. For example, Appendix M (the deck construction part) of the North Carolina State Residential Code is significantly different from the deck construction part of the International Residential Code (IRC) issued by the ICC.

- **Building codes are subject to interpretation, and the only people authorized to interpret building codes are government-authorized building officials.** Individual building officials in the same jurisdiction sometimes interpret and enforce building code provisions differently from other building officials in the same jurisdiction. This is not supposed to happen, but it does.

- **Building code organizations were regional before the early-2000s.** Before the ICC was founded in the mid-1990s, and before the first of the ICC's I-Codes were issued in the early-2000s, the model building code adopted by a government depended on where the government was located. The building codes issued by the regional code organizations were different, sometimes significantly so. We will refer to these regional codes in this book as the legacy codes. It is not practical, therefore, to determine code compliance at a national level when evaluating older decks.

- **Building codes change over time.** Building codes adapt, sometimes slowly, to new construction techniques and materials, advances in knowledge about construction science and technology, and evolving assessment of safety risks. The ICC revises most of its building codes on a three-year cycle. The most current IRC version as of the publication of this book is 2018.

- **Local jurisdictions usually take at least one year, and sometimes much longer, to adopt a new building code edition.** For example, a deck built in 2020 could be built under IRC 2012, or even an earlier edition.

- **Building codes provided minimal guidance about deck construction until about 2009.** Editions of the IRC up to and including the 2006 edition contained only a short paragraph about deck construction as part of a section about <u>**interior**</u> floor construction. IRC 2009 was the first regular edition that contained more guidance about deck construction, and this was mostly concerning deck ledger attachment to the structure. Even the most current IRC edition (2018) lacks specific guidance about important safety issues, such as guard post attachment to the deck. Lack of specific guidance allows significantly different code interpretations and enforcement between jurisdictions, and among building officials.
- **Many decks are built without a building permit, without code inspections, and without code enforcement.** Decks are often built by homeowners, and by carpenters who want to make some extra money on the weekends. The level of skill, knowledge, and care exercised by these people varies significantly.
- **The IRC and other deck construction guidelines apply to single-level decks that are wider than they are deep.** Multi-level decks, very tall decks (more than about 14 feet above the ground), and decks that are covered by a roof are examples of decks that should be designed and built by a qualified professional.

WHEN WAS THAT REQUIREMENT ADDED?

Answering the "when required" question, and answering the building code compliance question, is difficult at best. There are too many variables to consider, as discussed in the previous section. Besides, these questions miss the far more important point. **If the deck is currently unsafe, does it matter if it was building code compliant when the deck was built, or if a particular construction technique was required, or even just recommended, when the deck was built?** The answer is, or at least should be: **NO, it does not matter**.

WHAT IS UNSAFE?

Assuming that deck safety is the objective, then how does one define what is unsafe? The definition of unsafe as it relates to evaluating decks, or to evaluating any other building system or component, is subject to interpretation. The definition of unsafe used by the American Society of Home Inspectors (ASHI) is useful in this context:

(An unsafe condition is) a condition in a readily accessible, installed system or component that is judged by the inspector to be a significant risk of serious bodily injury during normal, day-to-day use; the risk may be due to damage, deterioration, improper installation, or a change in accepted residential construction practices.

This definition presents several concepts about which additional explanation may be helpful.

- What constitutes a **significant risk** is a judgment call. The judgment is based on factors such as: the overall condition of the deck, the type of defect, and the seriousness of the injury that could result if component failure were to occur. Reasonable people can reach different conclusions about what constitutes a significant risk.

- **Serious bodily injury** involves an injury that requires medical attention. This, too, is a judgment call. Many deck defects can, under the right conditions, result in a failure that could cause serious bodily injury.

- **Normal day-to-day use** means what it says. Misuse, abuse, and activities that create conditions beyond the those used to design and construct the deck are not included in this definition of unsafe. For example, a large number of people moving in unison, as could occur while dancing might not be considered normal day-to-day use. These activities, however, do occur on decks, and can cause a deck collapse. For example, a large number of people concentrated in a one area of the deck also might not be considered normal day-to-day use. This situation might occur when people assemble near the deck guard rail to take a group photograph, or to admire the view.

- **Conditions that are unrelated to compliance with building codes and deck construction guidelines can create an unsafe condition.** Damage and natural deterioration that occur when wood and metal are exposed to the elements can create an unsafe condition in what may once have been a building code compliant deck.

- **There is no grandfathering of safety issues.** Grandfathering is a term used to describe the fact that there is no general requirement to update an existing deck to current building code requirements. IRC Section R102.7, however, allows the building official to require upgrades for the general safety and welfare of the occupants and the public. Therefore, it does not matter if a deck was building code compliant or safe when it was built. **What matters is whether the deck is safe now.**

BUILDING CODES VERSUS BEST PRACTICES

As previously discussed, building codes set a minimum standard that is not intended to be best practice. **A deck can, therefore, be unsafe and be building code compliant at the same time.** Best practices are intended to make a deck as safe as possible when the best practices are properly implemented.

For decks, the most current sources of best practices as of the date of publication of this book are:

- **DCA 6-2015** published by the American Wood Council, and
- **manufacturer's installation instructions** for hardware including joist hangers, brackets, connectors, and fasteners.

DCA is an acronym meaning Design for Code Acceptance. A deck built according to DCA 6-2015 should not only be building code compliant, it should also be as safe as possible. DCA 6-2015 is much more comprehensive than the IRC when describing specific deck construction practices. **(DCA 6-2015 is a free download that you may find at https://www.awc.org/codes-standards/publications/dca6.)**

Compliance with manufacturer's installation instructions is not just a best practice. Compliance is at least an implied requirement of building codes, and can be considered a requirement.

LOCAL BUILDING CODES VERSUS BEST PRACTICES

Best practices sometimes go beyond the local building code to fill in the blanks where the local building code does not address an issue with a specific requirement. There are, however, confusing situations, such as: (1) when the local building code contradicts best practice, or (2) when the local building code allows materials or methods that are different from best practices, or (3) when the construction method or materials were allowed at one time, but are no longer allowed. How does one deal with these situations?

As previously discussed, if the situation creates a clear unsafe condition, then action to address it is appropriate. Such action may require a discussion with the local building official about what will be allowed. The situation is more complex if there is no clear unsafe condition.

Absent a clear unsafe condition, or visible evidence of component damage or deterioration, it seems reasonable to rely on the local building code to determine what is acceptable in that jurisdiction.

Many building departments provide examples of recommendations. The Cobb County Development and Inspections Division (https://www.cobbcounty.org/community-development/development-and-inspections/building-safety) has an excellent guide that goes beyond the minimum standards and emphasizes these important points:

1. average life expectancy of a wood deck,
2. the importance of regular deck inspections, and
3. the importance of hiring licensed professionals.

Many other building departments are trying to help the public understand the importance of best practices. Chesterfield County, Virginia, for example, has a wealth of information on its website.

FOR HOMEOWNERS

Decks are often undertaken as a do-it-yourself (DIY) project. Given correct attention to modern design specifications and workmanship, this can be a fine project for homeowners. A lack of knowledge, however, can lead to disaster. In fact, deck failure can cause serious injury or death. Decks are often the weakest structural component in the home. Dr. Don Bender, Weyerhaeuser Professor, Washington State University.

This section is primarily to help homeowners who may have limited experience in construction, and limited understanding of the conditions under which decks are often built. In order to perform a more accurate deck evaluation, it is necessary to understand the components that comprise the deck system, and to understand how those components are assembled. It also helps to understand terms that are often used when discussing decks. For this reason, you will find terms used in this book in the glossary.

In this section we will make a few important points about construction of older decks. We will then discuss the two ways that decks are typically added to a home: decks built during new construction, and decks added or replaced. But first, we will discuss older decks.

Construction of Older Decks

Until the middle 1990s to the late 2000s decks were considered simple structures that did not require much skill or planning to build. Some decks are still built as described below, especially in less populated areas where building code enforcement is limited or non-existent.

A deck builder, who could be a homeowner, would have a lumber yard deliver a deck lumber package, a couple boxes of nails, and a few bags of concrete. The deck builder would enlist some people to help, and in a few hours, there would be a deck. Although many jurisdictions required a permit to build a deck, this requirement was often ignored, especially when a deck was added to an existing building, or when a deck was replaced.

Decks were often built using what we now know are not best practices. Deck ledgers were nailed through wall coverings, and little or no thought was given to the type of or condition of the rim joist to which the deck ledger was nailed. Flashing at the deck ledger was an afterthought, if it was installed at all. Footings were installed by digging a hole, filling it with a bag of concrete, adding water, and sticking the post into the wet concrete. Stairs were nailed to the deck rim joist with as little as a couple inches of the stringers bearing on the rim joist. Everything was attached using nails that were often galvanized, but may or may not have had some type of deformed shank. Luck is a significant reason why more of these decks did not fail.

Thanks to work done at universities such as Virginia Tech and Washington State, and to efforts by forward-thinking code officials such as those in Fairfax County, Virginia, we now know that decks are more complex systems that require skill and planning to build. Beginning in the middle 2000s, deck building best practices and deck-specific building codes have become better defined and more widely available. Code enforcement has become more rigorous.

Decks Built During New Construction

In new building construction, the building plans should specify where the decks will be located. Plans for the deck should be submitted for approval by the building official along with the building plans that are submitted when the building permit is pulled. Ideally, code officials will inspect the deck as part of the permit inspection process.

Deck construction can be coordinated with the construction of a new building. The building plans should specify that an approved rim board be installed where the deck will be located. The builder can ensure that flashing is installed where appropriate before deck construction begins. The builder can ensure that wall coverings are omitted where the decks will be located. Installation of proper footings can be coordinated with a scheduled concrete delivery, such as when the driveway is installed. Constructing a well-built deck during new building construction should be relatively easy.

Decks Added or Replaced

Adding a deck to an existing building, or replacing a deck that is at the end of its service life, is a more complex process than building a deck for a new building. Wall coverings will need to be removed if this has not occurred. Removing wall coverings such as brick veneer and stucco can be difficult, and can create both structural problems and water intrusion problems.

A self-supporting deck (similar terms include free-standing deck and non-ledger deck) is often a good option if removing wall coverings is not practical. In addition, it may be more difficult to integrate deck flashing into the wall drainage system when adding or replacing a deck, especially at doors that open onto the deck. So, again, a self-supporting or free-standing (non-ledger) deck may be a better option.

Providing adequate footings can be a challenge, especially if an existing deck has inadequate footings, or if there is a thin (usually 3½ inches thick) patio slab where the deck footings will be. Removal of any existing concrete is usually difficult, as is hand-mixing multiple bags of concrete.

One may need to deal with adverse existing conditions, especially when adding a new deck. Large trees may be in the way. Removing a large tree near a deck can be expensive. Building around or very close to trees is usually not a good plan because as the tree grows it may damage the deck. In addition, if the tree moves during a storm, it may damage the deck or drop large limbs on the deck.

There are several other factors to consider. Deck construction may damage the tree and cause it to die. Air conditioning condensers may be located under where the deck is to be built. Many manufacturers recommend leaving clearance of at least one foot around a condenser and three feet above the condenser. Overhead electricity service cables or broadband cable may be located near where the deck is to be built. These cables should be at least ten feet above and at least three feet horizontally from a deck.

Additional adverse existing conditions include grade of the ground where the deck will be located. Decks built very close to the soil may deteriorate more rapidly because the wood and the hardware may be subjected to constant moisture. It can also be difficult to manage water under and around low decks so that the water flows away from the building. A patio may be a better option to a low deck, given these potential issues.

Very tall decks can be a challenge to build because of the need to build temporary scaffolding to access the deck during construction, and to build temporary support for the deck. Posts that are taller than fourteen feet above the deck footing may need to be designed by an engineer.

SAFETY FIRST – A CASE STUDY

Throughout this chapter, we have tried to emphasize that what matters is whether the deck is safe today. When the deck was built, whether the deck complied with code when it was built, and even the condition of the deck are secondary considerations. A brief case study may be instructive.

Sometime around 2018, a building official purchased a home with a deck that was built in 2004. Exercising extraordinary due diligence, the building official had the deck inspected by his home inspector and by a structural engineer. The verdict: the deck was in acceptable condition given its age, and given the standards in effect when it was built. Whether the deck was safe was a different question.

Being a building official, he was more aware than most about the potential risks of having an unsafe deck. For the safety of his family, friends, and guests, he decided to have the deck demolished and replaced with a deck built according to DCA 6-2015. This was probably at least a $10,000 decision.

Was the decision extreme? Perhaps.

Everyone must make their own calculation about how to balance safety and financial considerations. The fact that a building official decided to make this costly investment in deck safety speaks volumes, and is worthy of your consideration.

2: DECK FLASHING

OVERVIEW

Repeated exposure to water can damage wood, including preservative-treated wood. Wood preservative treatment is only a tiny fraction of an inch thick layer on the outside of the wood. The rest of the wood under that thin layer of preservative treatment is regular untreated wood. Every cut in the wood, and every penetration of the wood by a fastener, is a place where water can enter and damage the wood.

It does not take much water damage to weaken wood to the point where the wood, or the fasteners embedded in the wood, can fail. It does not matter how many fasteners are installed in water-damaged wood; the fasteners are likely to fail, such as by withdrawing from the water-damaged wood. In addition, repeated exposure to water can increase the rate at which metal hardware (e. g., fasteners, joist hangers, brackets, connectors) corrodes (rusts). Corrosion can cause the hardware to fail. Water-damaged wood, corrosion, or both, can cause a deck failure.

Properly installed deck flashing helps reduce water infiltration at the deck ledger board and at wall penetrations to the deck, such as at doors. Deck flashing is, therefore, essential to keeping the deck system intact and safe to use. Deck flashing is also essential to help keep the building to which the deck is attached free from water damage, and free from a potential mold infestation.

IMPLICATIONS OF DECK FLASHING FAILURE

The primary implications of deck flashing failure are deck ledger board detachment (and a deck failure), water damage to the building, and potential mold infestation resulting from water infiltration into the building. Deck ledger board detachment is uncommon relative to the total number of decks in service, but the implication drawn from previous cases of deck ledger board detachment is that this failure can include fatalities, injury, and property damage. Inadequate deck flashing may be considered an unsafe condition.

Figure 11

Note the deteriorated rim joist shown below this sliding door. Imagine what would happen if the deck that was attached to this rim joist were higher off the ground.

GENERAL DECK FLASHING REQUIREMENTS

DCA 6 cites the IRC flashing requirement which provides locations where flashing should be installed, and prescribes one type of deck flashing material. The IRC flashing requirement is, however, primarily a performance requirement. This means that the IRC requirement is that water should not penetrate into the building. Neither DCA 6 nor the IRC provide details about how to install deck flashing.

The two most vulnerable locations for water infiltration into the building at a deck are at the deck ledger board, and at wall penetrations, such as doors from the house to the deck. Properly installed deck flashing at the deck ledger board should be integrated into the building wall water-resistive barrier to form a drainage plane that diverts water which flows behind the deck ledger board. This flashing also provides a path for the water to drain and to not enter the building. Properly installed wall penetration (door) flashing should be integrated into the building wall water-resistive barrier, and into the deck ledger board flashing. This is in order to divert water which flows through, around, or under the wall penetration and should provide a path for the water to drain and not enter the building. Refer to Figures 12 and 13.

2: Deck Flashing   23

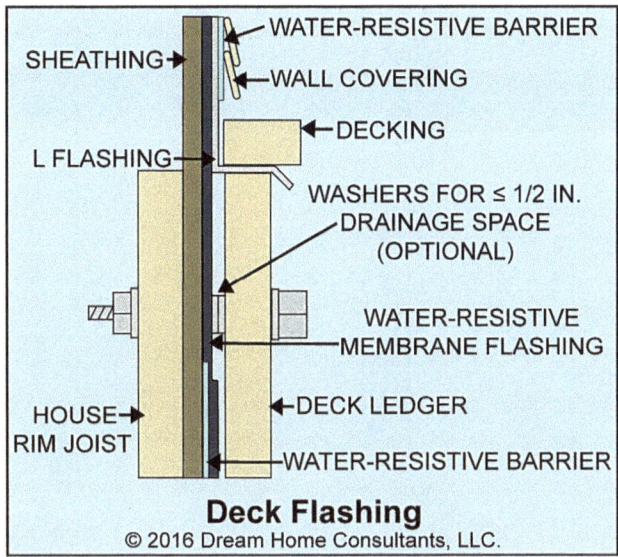

Figure 12

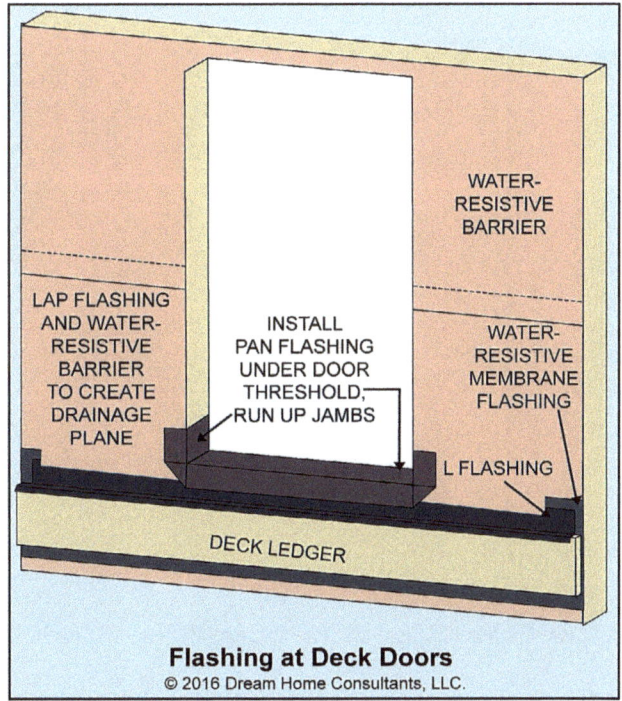

Figure 13

Note how flashing is installed to stop water from entering the building at vulnerable locations, and to provide water with a path to drain out. Upper layers are lapped above lower layers so that water does not enter at the seams between them.

2: Deck Flashing

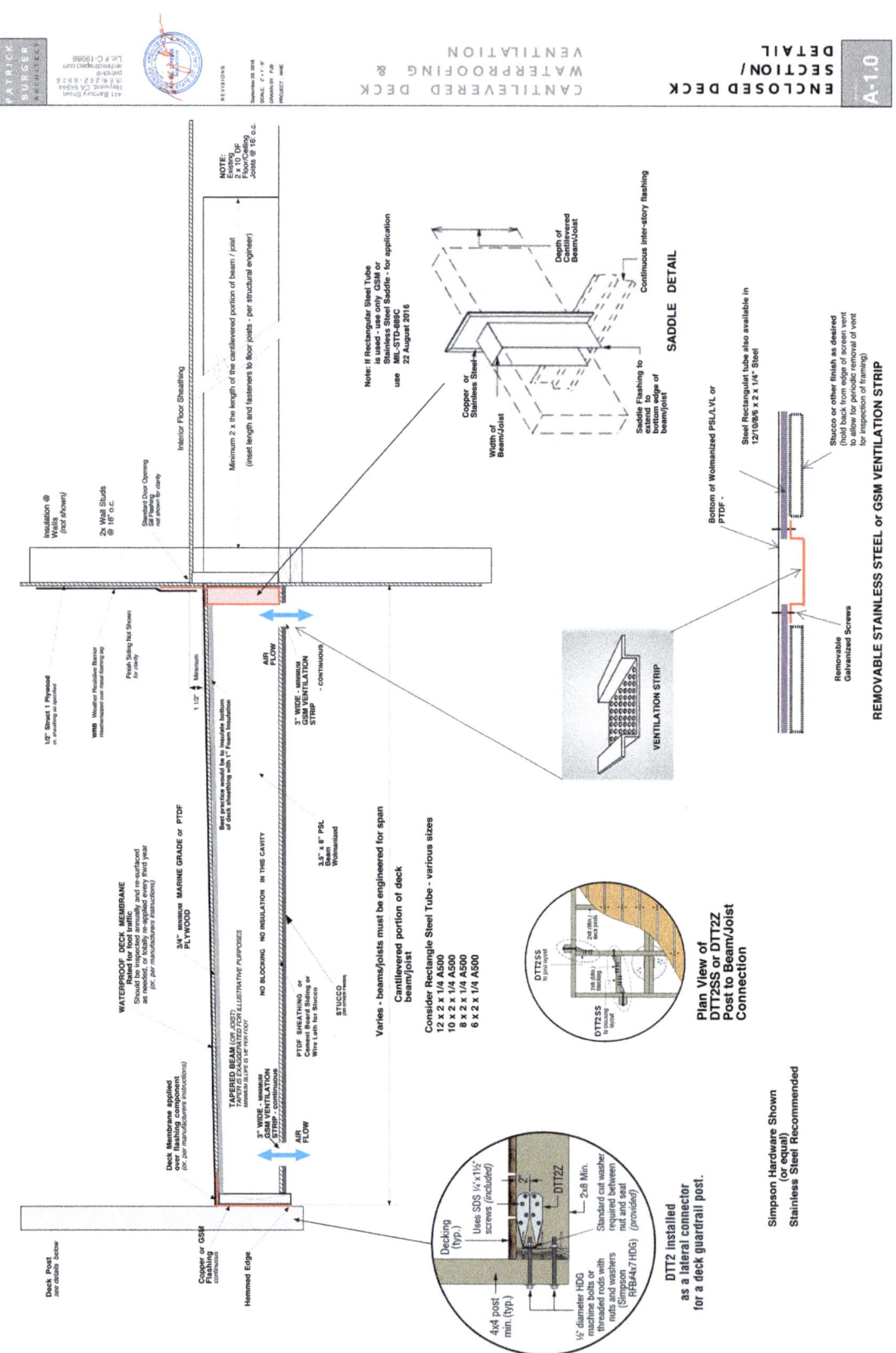

Figure 14 courtesy of Patrick Berger

As seen in Figure 14, flashing balconies, especially cantilevered balconies, is challenging. This illustration shows one good way to install flashing. Flashing and ventilation are essential, especially when the balcony is covered on both the top and the bottom.

HISTORY

The general requirement to install deck flashing has been in the IRC since the 1998 edition (R703.8). The requirement has not changed significantly since that time. Current IRC 2018 flashing requirements are in R507.2.4, R703.1.1, and R703.4.

2.1 - DEFECT – ABSENT, IMPROPERLY INSTALLED, DAMAGED, AND DETERIORATED DECK FLASHING

Editorial note: chapters following chapter two have multiple defects listed. This chapter includes only 2.1 as shown.

The most significant occurrence of this defect involves lack of flashing at the deck ledger board, and lack of flashing at doors and other penetrations that open onto the deck. Less significant occurrences of this defect include gaps or openings in the flashing, use of materials that are not approved for use as deck flashing (such as using aluminum flashing with decks built after 2004), damaged and significantly deteriorated flashing, and use of incompatible materials (such as securing stainless steel flashing with galvanized steel). Note that flashing details may not be fully visible for evaluation.

Absent, improperly installed, damaged, and deteriorated deck flashing increases the risk of deck failure. The primary reason is that water can infiltrate behind the deck ledger board or around wall penetrations. It can also damage deck or building components, and can create conditions whereby the hardware that holds the deck system together withdraws or deteriorates. This can cause deck failure. Absent or improperly installed deck flashing also increases the risk of damage to the building for the same reasons. This damage can become significant and can require costly repairs.

Absent, improperly installed, damaged, and deteriorated deck flashing may create an unsafe condition. Action to correct the situation should be recommended. Closer inspection of hardware, the deck ledger board, and the building band joist/rim board condition is prudent. Repair of this defect depends on the situation.

2: Deck Flashing

Proper installation of flashing may require removal of wall coverings and doors to allow integration of the flashing into the wall drainage plane. Note that application of sealants, such as caulk, is not an adequate substitute for flashing.

Figure 15

Note the gap between the black flashing and the door threshold. Water will enter the building through this gap. The flashing should have been turned under the threshold as shown in this figure.

Figure 16

This is what it looked like in the crawlspace under the door in Figure 15. Note the stained floor sheathing, the rusted nails, and the rusted bolt.

Figure 17

Look inside the red box. What do you see? What do you not see? What you see is oriented strand board sheathing. What you do not see is flashing. Water will enter the building through this unflashed area.

Figure 18 courtesy of Jerrod Turnbow

The L-flashing above the deck ledger should extend further beyond the ledger, and should turn down over the ledger to limit water intrusion under the ledger. We hope that the flashing installed behind the ledger is properly integrated into the water-resistative barrier of the wall.

Figure 19

The deterioration of this floor truss was caused by water entering the building because there was no flashing between the deck and this area. This stems from thirty years of damage and addressing it will be costly. This is thirty years of damage.

Figure 20

Sometimes it does not take long for damage to appear. This is wall sheathing in the crawlspace under a one year old deck.

3: DECK ATTACHMENT TO THE BUILDING

OVERVIEW

Most decks are supported on one end by attaching the deck to the building. This is usually done by fastening a deck ledger board to the building as shown in Figures 21 and 22. One must exercise care when fastening a deck ledger board to a building to ensure that it does not detach from the building and contribute to a deck collapse.

The deck ledger board must resist three primary loads: vertical (gravity), horizontal (lateral), and uplift. The **vertical load tries to pull the deck down**. The **horizontal load tries to pull the deck away from the house**, then gravity takes over and pulls the deck down. Fasteners and connectors must be installed to resist both loads. Deck ledger boards, and the attached deck floor joists, must also resist the load caused by joist uplift. This **uplift load** is most common when deck floor joists are cantilevered beyond the supporting beam. Refer to Figure 23.

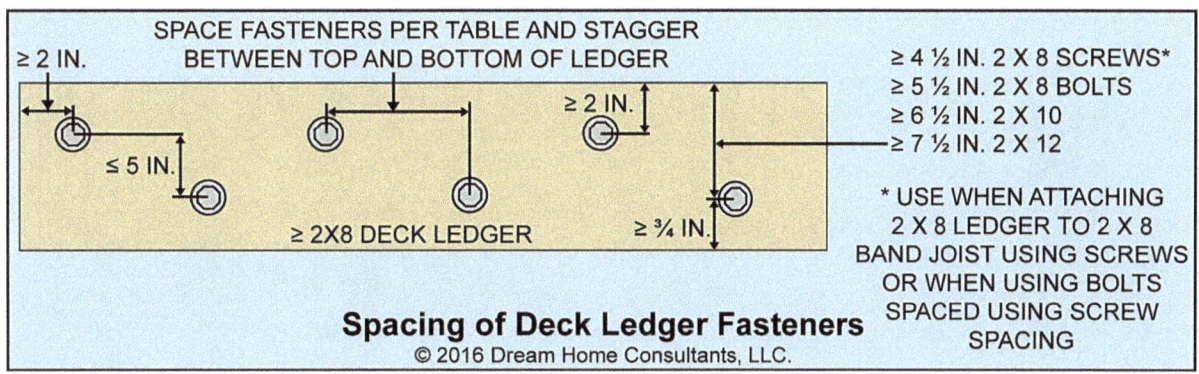

Figure 21

Note that fastener spacing in Figures 21 and 22 assume ½-inch diameter bolts or screws. Fastener spacing will increase if larger bolts and screws are used. Spacing for listed manufactured deck ledger screws is per the screw manufacturer's instructions.

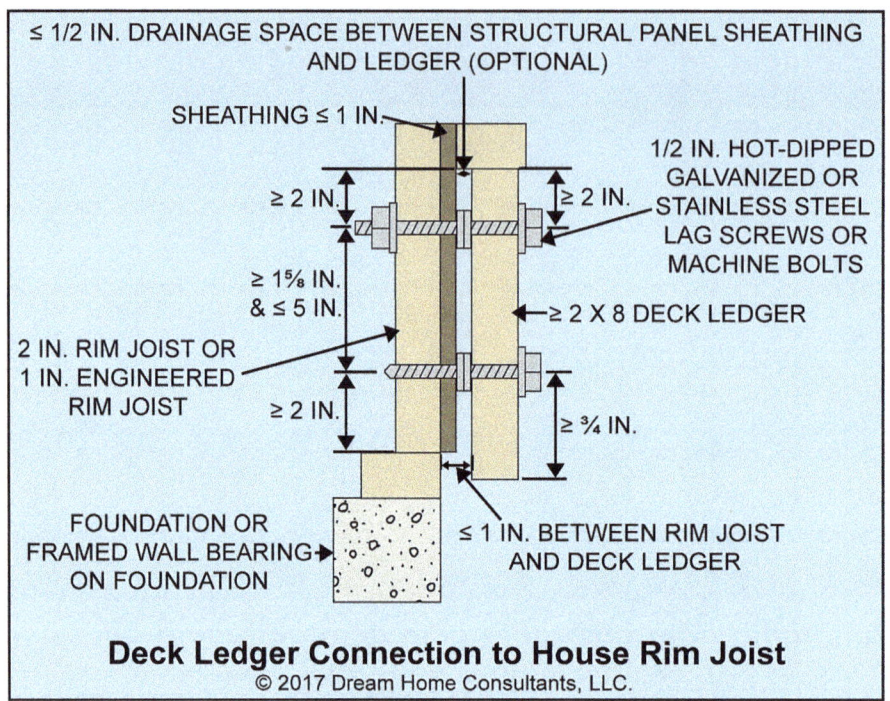

Figure 22

Note the spacing between the fasteners, and between the fasteners and the edges of the wood.

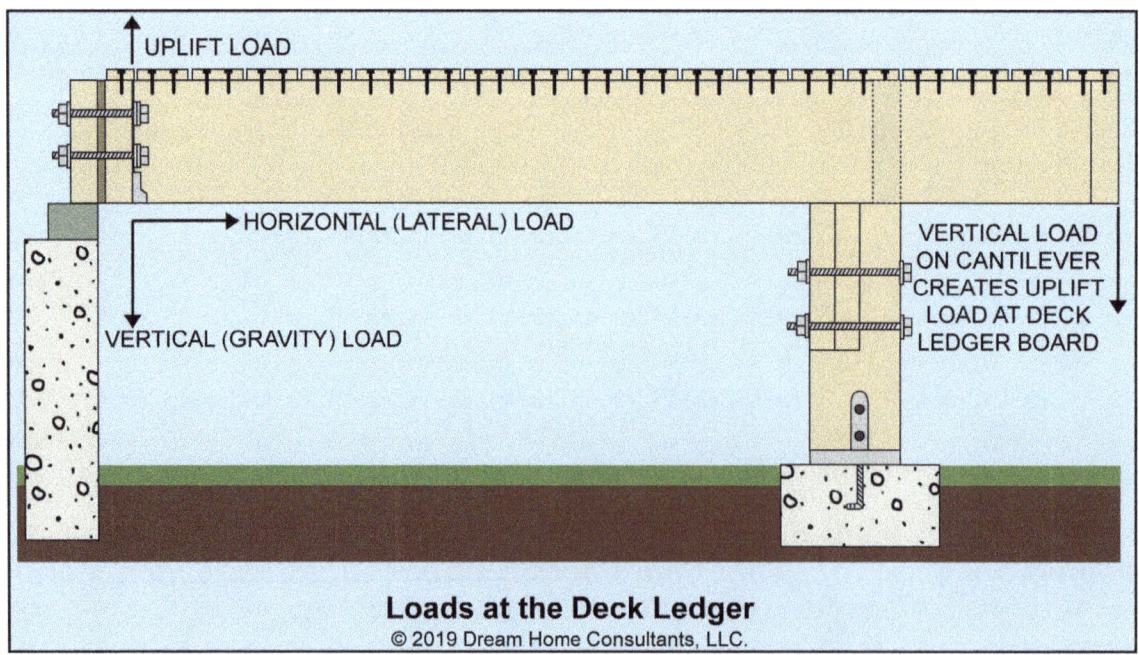

Figure 23

Machine bolts or screws that attach the deck ledger board are installed primarily to resist the vertical and uplift loads. **While bolts or screws provide some horizontal load resistance, determining if the horizontal load resistance is adequate requires an engineering analysis of the deck.** It is usually more efficient, and less expensive, to install lateral load connectors to resist the horizontal load.

IMPLICATIONS OF DECK LEDGER BOARD DETACHMENT

The implications of deck ledger board detachment can include fatalities, injury, and property damage. Inadequate attachment of the deck ledger board to the building should, therefore, be considered an unsafe condition.

GENERAL DECK LEDGER BOARD ATTACHMENT REQUIREMENTS

Attaching the deck ledger board to the building involves fastening a preservative-treated deck ledger board to a dimensional lumber band joist, or to an at least 1-inch thick engineered wood rim board. The band joist or rim board must bear on the building foundation, or on a wall that bears on the building foundation. Fastening through wall sheathing up to 1-inch thick is allowed. Fastening through wall coverings is prohibited; however, fastening through brick veneer is allowed in some jurisdictions.

Fasteners that attach the deck ledger board to the building should be hot-dipped galvanized steel, or stainless steel, machine bolts or screws that are at least ½-inch diameter, and that have washers installed on the head and nut ends. Carriage bolts may not be substituted for machine bolts. Refer to Figure 24. Fastener quantity and spacing depends on factors such as fastener type (bolt or screw), sheathing thickness, and deck floor joist length. Refer to Figures 21 and 22.

34   3: Deck Attachment to the Building

Figure 24

Carriage bolts like this may not be substituted for machine bolts. Reasons include weakened and damaged wood if the carriage bolt is installed without a washer, and water intrusion if the carriage bolt is installed with a washer, as shown in this picture.

Bolts and screws are installed primarily to resist the vertical load. **Lateral load connectors (also called tension ties) should also be installed,** in most cases, to resist the horizontal load. Refer to Figures 25 through 28. Other fasteners may be used to resist the vertical load, such as those from Simpson Strong-Tie and LedgerLok. These fasteners must be installed according to the manufacturer's instructions.

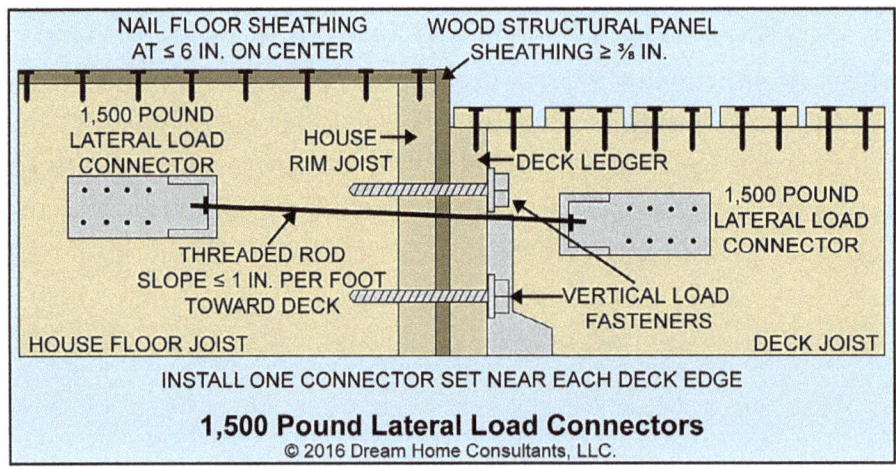

Figure 25

This illustrates a lateral load connection using a Simpson DTT2, or a similar tension tie, and threaded rod. Note the interior floor sheathing fastener requirement at the top left of the illustration.

3: Deck Attachment to the Building 35

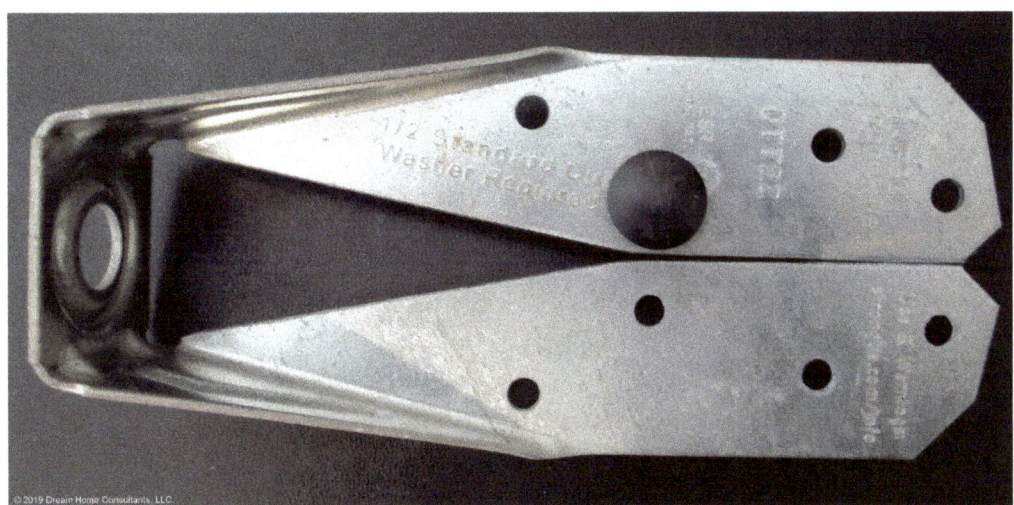

Figure 26

Picture of a Simpson Strong-Tie DTT2. This tension-tie connector is also used to secure deck guard posts. Refer to Chapter 4.

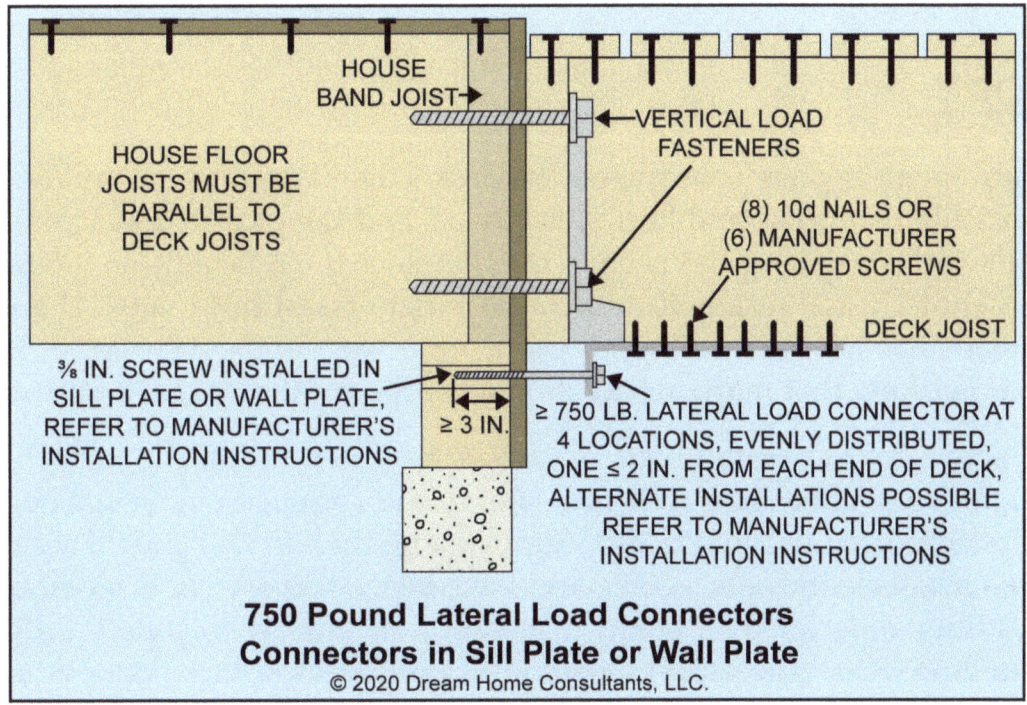

Figure 27

This illustrates a lateral load connection using a Simpson DTT1 or a similar tension tie. Note that the house floor joists must be parallel to the deck joists in order to use this type of tension tie.

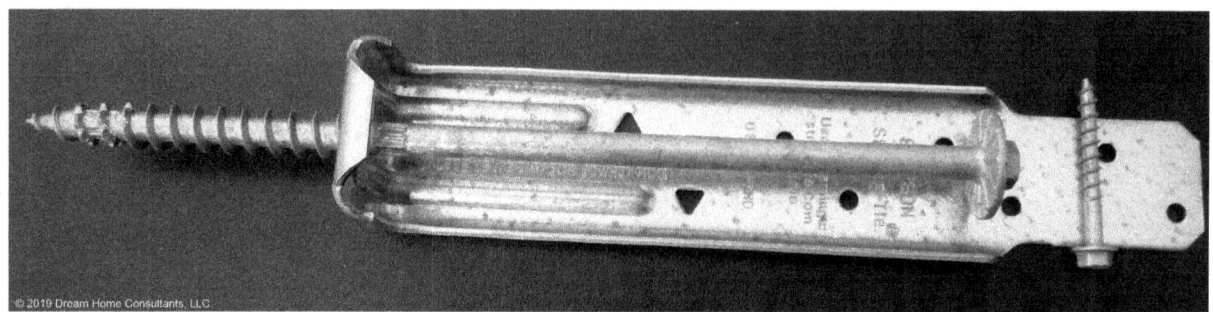

Figure 28

Picture of a Simpson Strong-Tie DTT1.

Other fastening methods to resist the vertical load may be acceptable, although they are not specifically addressed in the IRC. Attachment to floor truss end chords may be acceptable when installed according to guidelines from the Structural Building Components Association. Attachment to foundation walls made from concrete and from fully-grouted concrete masonry unit (concrete block) may be acceptable when the fasteners are installed according to the fastener manufacturer's instructions.

HISTORY

The requirement to positively anchor the deck ledger board to the building in order to resist both vertical and horizontal loads, and the prohibition against using only nails as the fasteners, has been in the IRC since the 2000 edition (R502.2). The requirement to install fasteners and connectors to **resist both vertical and horizontal loads** has not been well understood, and has not been enforced. **Because of this, it is likely that many decks do not comply with the IRC requirement.**

Details about how to install bolts or screws to fasten the deck ledger board to the building, and about how to install lateral load connectors to resist horizontal loads, first appeared in the IRC 2007 Supplement, then in IRC 2009. These details were also available in DCA 6-2006, and have been in every DCA 6 edition since then. Additional deck ledger board installation details are included in IRC 2012, 2015, and 2018 (R507 since 2015). Current IRC 2018 deck ledger board attachment requirements are in R507.8 and R507.9.

3.1 - DEFECT – NAILED OR SCREWED DECK LEDGER BOARD

A deck ledger board that is attached to the building using only nails, or using only screws that are not listed for attaching a deck ledger board, significantly increases the risk of deck ledger board detachment and of deck collapse. Refer to Figures 21, 22, 29 and 30. The reasons include:

- nails and unlisted screws can withdraw from wood, especially when attached through wall coverings; and
- nails and unlisted screws may break (shear) under the vertical load imposed by the deck.

Figure 29

Figure 30

A deck ledger board may not be attached to the building using only nails or only unlisted screws, especially when attached to or through wall covering.

A deck ledger board that is attached to the building using only nails or unlisted screws creates a significant unsafe condition. Immediate action to correct this defect should be recommended.

The safety concern is increased when this defect is combined with other defects, such as attachment through wall coverings, attachment to unapproved components (such as I-joists and sheathing), and inadequate deck flashing. Nails and unlisted screws attached through wall covering may have little, if any, penetration into solid wood, and the wood may be damaged by water penetration.

3.2 - DEFECT – DECK LEDGER BOARD ATTACHED THROUGH WALL COVERINGS

A deck ledger board that is attached to the building through wall coverings increases the risk of deck ledger board detachment. Refer to Figures 31 and 32. The reasons include:

- the additional distance between the deck ledger board and the building causes the fasteners to break (shear), especially when attached through thick wall coverings such as brick; and
- attachment through wall coverings can make flashing installation more difficult, increasing the chance of wood deterioration and fastener withdrawal.

A deck ledger board attached to the building through wall coverings may create an unsafe condition. The risk depends on factors such as the type of wall covering, the condition of the deck ledger board, the condition of the band joist or rim board, and the type and condition of the fasteners. Evaluation of the deck ledger board attachment should be recommended.

Repair of this defect depends on the situation. Removing the deck ledger board, removing the wall covering, and reattaching the deck ledger board may be possible. Converting the deck to a free-standing deck may be possible. There are no IRC-approved methods of attaching a deck ledger board through wall coverings. Analysis of the deck ledger board attachment by an engineer will likely be necessary in order to design a reliable deck ledger board attachment if the deck ledger board and the wall covering are left in place.

3: Deck Attachment to the Building   39

Figure 31

Figure 32

A deck ledger board may not be attached through wall covering, such as the siding in the top picture and the brick veneer in the bottom picture. Fasteners that attach the deck ledger board in the top picture are not approved for attaching a deck ledger board. Fasteners that attach the deck ledger board in the bottom picture may not be attached through brick veneer, and the fasteners are improperly spaced. Also note the improper use of deck screws to attach the joist hangers.

3.3 - DEFECT – IMPROPER DECK LEDGER BOARD FASTENER TYPE OR QUANTITY

Deck ledger board fastener type and quantity defects include failure to install (1) the approved type of fasteners, (2) the required nuts and washers, or (3) the required quantity of fasteners. Refer to Figures 21, 22, 33 and 34. Refer to the General Deck Ledger Board Attachment Requirements section for additional information.

Deck ledger board fastener type and quantity defects increase the risk of deck ledger detachment. The primary reason is that there may not be enough fasteners to keep the deck ledger board from detaching and contributing to a deck collapse.

A deck ledger board attached to the building using improper fastener type or quantity may create an unsafe condition. The risk depends on factors such as (1) the diameter and the type of fasteners, (2) the quantity and location of fasteners, (3) the condition of the deck ledger board, (4) the condition of the building band joist or rim board, and (5) the condition of the fasteners.

Evaluation of the deck ledger board attachment should be recommended. Repair of this defect can be easy or difficult, depending on the conditions encountered.

Figure 33

This picture presents several defects. Carriage bolts are improperly used as deck ledger board fasteners. The hole around the carriage bolt is too large. The joist hanger flanges are not tight against the joist. Thin gun-driven nails appear to have been used to secure joist hangers. The deck ledger board is improperly attached through brick veneer. Some joists are improperly supported using only nails.

Figure 34

This picture shows a bolt without a washer and a nut viewed from the crawlspace. There may have been a nut and washer on this bolt at one time. Also note that the bolt is too close to the edge of the band joist.

3.4 - DEFECT – IMPROPER DECK LEDGER BOARD FASTENER SPACING AND LOCATION

Deck ledger board fastener spacing and location defects include locating fasteners that are (1) too close to the edges of the deck ledger board, or (2) too close to the edges of the building band joist or rim board, or (3) too close to each other. Refer to Figures 21, 22, and 35. Deck ledger board fasteners should be staggered vertically, and not installed in a straight line. Refer to Figures 21 and 36.

Deck ledger board fastener spacing and location defects increase the risk of deck ledger board detachment. The primary reason is that the deck ledger board may split if the fasteners are not located in the recommended locations. A split deck ledger board could contribute to deck ledger board detachment from the building, and a deck collapse.

A deck ledger board attached to the building with improperly spaced or located fasteners is usually at a low risk for being an unsafe condition, assuming that there is no visible evidence of wood damage. Regular monitoring of the deck ledger board, and of the band joist/rim board, should be recommended, assuming no visible evidence of wood damage.

Repair of this defect, if necessary, usually involves installing additional fasteners.

42   3: Deck Attachment to the Building

Figure 35

The fasteners at the right are too close to the top edge of the deck ledger board, and are improperly installed through brick veneer.

Figure 36

Fasteners should be staggered vertically as shown in this picture.

3.5 - DEFECT – BUILDING BAND JOIST OR RIM BOARD DOES NOT BEAR ON THE FOUNDATION

Attaching a deck ledger board to a building band joist or a rim board that does not bear on the foundation, or on a wall that bears on the foundation, is prohibited. This defect usually involves attaching the deck ledger board to a cantilevered projection, such as for a framed chimney chase, or for a bay window. Refer to Figures 37 and 38.

3: Deck Attachment to the Building

Attaching a deck ledger board to a building band joist or rim board that does not bear on the foundation increases the risk of deck ledger board detachment. This also increases the risk of building damage and deformation. The primary reason is that the cantilevered projection to which the deck ledger is attached is usually not designed to resist the vertical, horizontal, and uplift loads imposed by the deck. The cantilevered projection framing may deflect or detach under load and weaken the connection between the deck ledger board and the building. This could contribute to deck ledger board detachment, and a deck collapse.

A deck ledger board attached to a band joist or rim board that does not bear on the foundation creates an unsafe condition. Evaluation of the situation should be recommended.

Repair of this defect may include framing around the cantilevered projection by installing beams (trimmers) on each side of the projection, and installing a beam (header) between the beams to support the deck floor joists. Refer to Figure 39. Another repair option is to make the deck free-standing at the cantilevered structure.

Figure 37

This deck ledger board is improperly attached to a cantilevered projection, is fastened only with nails, and is improperly attached through wall covering.

Figure 38 courtesy of Jerrod Turnbow

This is another example of a deck ledger board that is improperly attached to a cantilevered projection.

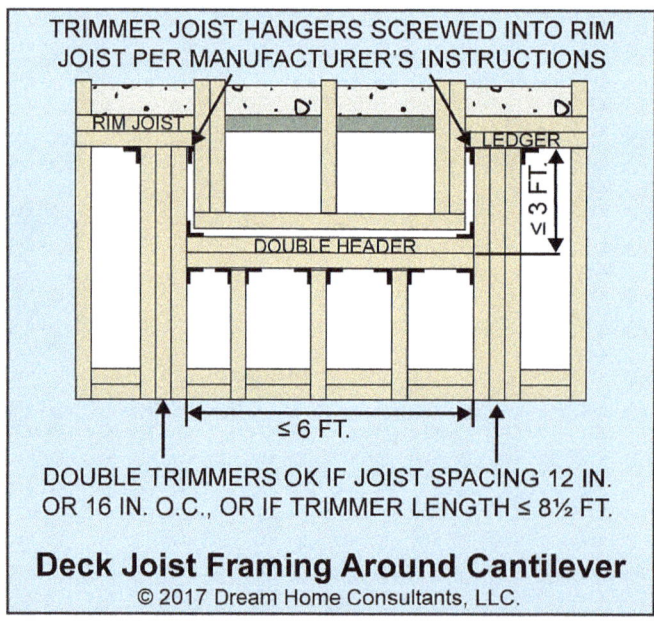

Figure 39

This illustration shows one method of dealing with a cantilevered projection. One may frame around the projection as illustrated. Note that the joist hangers supporting the trimmers are usually a special-order item. This joist hanger must be installed with manufacturer-recommended screws that penetrate into the house band joist or rim board.

3.6 - DEFECT – DECK LEDGER BOARD NOT ATTACHED TO AN APPROVED COMPONENT

This defect involves attaching a deck ledger board to components such as I-joists, wall sheathing, or rim boards that are less than 1-inch thick. Refer to Figures 21 and 22 and Figures 40 and 44. Variants include installing bolts or screws through wood blocks that bear on the unapproved components, and improperly installing bolts or screws at floor trusses and foundation walls. Refer to Figures 41, 42, and 43.

As indicated in the General Deck Ledger Attachment Requirements section, a deck ledger board may be attached to floor trusses, and may be attached to foundations, such as fully-grouted concrete blocks and cast-in-place concrete. Attachment to other components, such as wood-framed wall plates and studs, may be acceptable, but this would require evaluation by an engineer.

Attaching a deck ledger board to an unapproved component increases the risk of deck ledger detachment, and creates an unsafe condition. The primary reason is that the unapproved component may not be able to resist the vertical, horizontal, and uplift loads imposed by the deck.

Engineer evaluation should be recommended.

Repair of this defect depends on the situation.

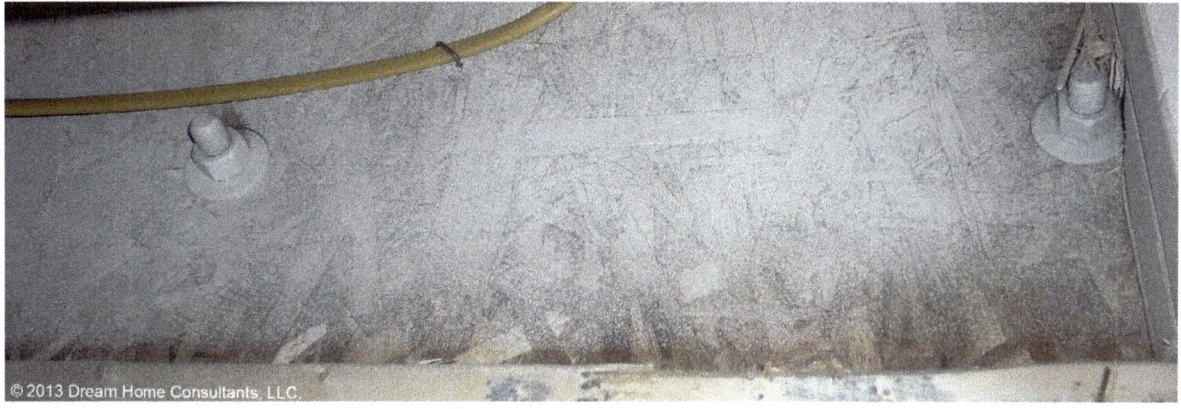

Figure 40

This deck ledger board is improperly attached to an I-joist rim board. Note that an I-joist web is often around ⅜-inch thick

3: Deck Attachment to the Building

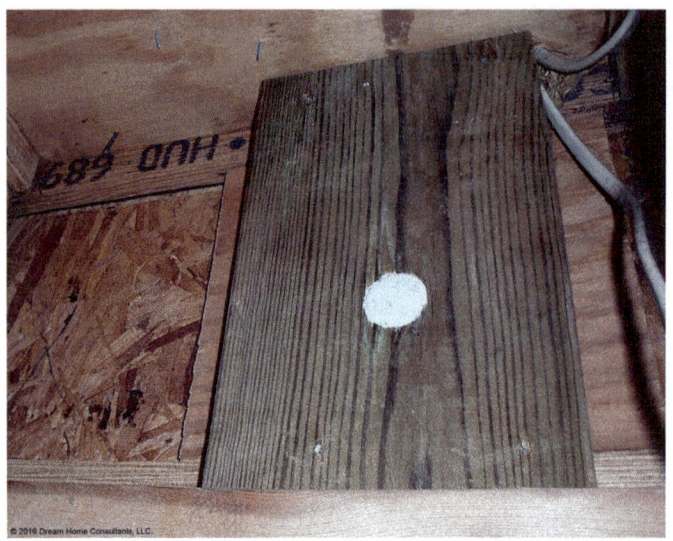

Figure 41

This deck ledger board is improperly attached to an I-joist rim board. The wood block does not make the attachment correct.

Figure 42

This deck ledger board is improperly attached to a rim truss.

Figure 43 courtesy of John Cauthen

This deck ledger board is improperly attached to a rim truss.

Figure 44

This deck ledger board is improperly attached to OSB wall sheathing.

3.7 - DEFECT – LATERAL LOAD CONNECTORS NOT INSTALLED

While it is possible for machine bolts that connect a deck ledger board to an approved band joist or rim board to provide the required lateral load resistance, **confirming this requires an engineering analysis of the deck.** The far less expensive option is to install lateral load connectors. Refer to Figures 25 through 28. The option to use lateral load connectors to provide the required lateral load resistance first appeared in IRC 2009.

Failure to install lateral load connectors may increase the risk of deck ledger board detachment. The primary reason is that the attachment system may not be able to resist the lateral (horizontal) loads imposed by the deck. The deck could pull away from the house, bringing the band joist or rim board along with it.

Lack of lateral load connectors may create an unsafe condition. Installation of lateral load connectors should be recommended, or an engineering analysis of the deck may be recommended as an alternative.

3.8 - DEFECT – DETERIORATED OR DAMAGED WOOD

Wood exposed to water, even preservative-treated wood and naturally durable wood, will eventually deteriorate. This is especially true for preservative-treated wood that has been cut or drilled. The cut and drilled area is untreated, unless field-treated with a preservative. Field treatment of cuts is required by the IRC, although doing so is very uncommon. Even a little deterioration can decrease the strength of the wood. Lack of adequate flashing can increase the opportunity for wood deterioration.

Deteriorated and damaged wood can be difficult to observe because much or all of the sheathing and band joist or rim board may be concealed. Visible evidence of possible wood deterioration may present first as water stains around fastener penetrations, or as red rust on fasteners. Refer to Figures 45 and 46.

Deteriorated and damaged wood increases the risk of deck ledger board detachment, thereby contributing to a deck collapse. The primary reason is that the wood may be weakened to the point where connection between the wood and the fastener may not be adequate to resist the loads imposed by the deck.

Deteriorated and damaged wood may create an unsafe condition. Evaluation of the deck ledger board, band joist/rim board, fasteners, and deck flashing should be recommended. Repair of this defect depends on the situation.

Figure 45

Figure 46

These are examples of deteriorated and damaged wood. Looks like something has been chewing on the 2 x 2 ledger strip in the lower picture. The deterioration and damage to the 2 x 2 ledger strips, and the likely deterioration of the nails that attach the ledger strip, increase the chance of ledger strip failure, and of a deck collapse.

Figure 47

This is a picture of red rust on a deck ledger board fastener. Note the water-stained wood that may indicate concealed wood deterioration.

3.9 - DEFECT – DETERIORATED HARDWARE

Deteriorated deck hardware (e. g., fasteners, joist hangers, brackets, and connectors) usually presents with white rust or red rust. White rust indicates that the zinc coating (galvanization) protecting the steel is deteriorating, and that the hardware is nearing the end of its service life. Red rust indicates that the steel is deteriorating, and that the hardware is near or at the end of its service life. Refer to Figures 49 and 50.

Fasteners presenting red rust may increase the risk of deck ledger detachment. The thickness and shear strength of the fastener may be compromised, and the wood around the fastener may also be compromised. These conditions may not be visible without removing the fastener. Figure 48 presents a good example of a compromised fastener. Other hardware presenting red rust may increase the risk of failure of the components secured to or supported by the hardware.

Hardware presenting with red rust may create an unsafe condition. Evaluation of the deck ledger board, the band joist or rim board, fasteners, and deck flashing, should be recommended. Hardware presenting with white rust does not create an unsafe condition. Regular monitoring of this hardware should be recommended.

Red-rusted hardware may need to be replaced. If wood deterioration is also an issue, hardware replacement by itself may not be adequate.

Figure 48

This picture shows what a deteriorated fastener (on the right) may look like inside of the wood, where you usually cannot see the fastener. Note the difference between the condition and thickness of the older fastener (top left) versus the newer fastener (bottom left).

Figure 49

This bolt, washer, and nut present white rust. The zinc galvanization coating is wearing away. Red rust will follow, indicating that the fastener is approaching the end of its service life.

Figure 50

This is a picture of significant red rust of the fasteners and the joist hangers. This hardware is past the end of its service life.

4: GUARDS AND HANDRAILS

OVERVIEW

Guards (often called guardrails) help prevent falls from a deck, or from the stairs serving the deck. Handrails exist to provide a graspable surface to help people safely use the stairs, and to help prevent falls while using the stairs. The opening size between guard fill-in components (often called balusters or pickets) helps prevent strangulation of a child if the head became trapped between the components, and helps prevent children from falling between the fill-in components.

IMPLICATIONS OF GUARD AND HANDRAIL FAILURE

Falls from decks caused by guard and handrail failure (detachment or collapse), and falls caused by lack of a graspable handrail, are one of the most common types of deck-related injuries. Because guard and handrail failure can result in fatalities and injury, improper guard and handrail installation and deteriorated guards and handrails are often unsafe conditions.

GENERAL GUARD AND HANDRAIL REQUIREMENTS

A guard is required whenever a walking surface (the deck and the stairway) is more than 30 inches vertically above any surface below, including above grade. The 30-inch vertical measurement is made at a point 36 inches horizontally from the walking surface. Refer to Figure 51.

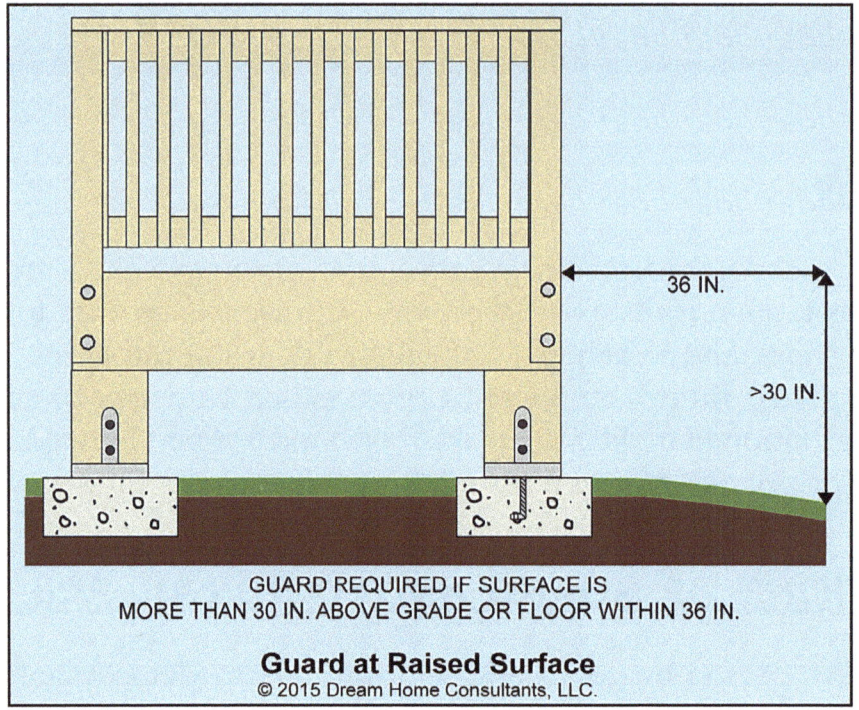

Figure 51

A guard may be any system that complies with the guard requirements. The most common system for deck guards is a preservative-treated wood post and vertical baluster system. Other guard systems include a solid wall, wood lattice, a post and wire cable system, and a system using glass panels as fill-in components.

A guard at a horizontal surface should be at least 36 inches tall measured vertically from the walking surface (the deck). Refer to Figure 52. The height is 42 inches in a few jurisdictions, such as California.

A guard at a stairway (stair guard) with a handrail on the top of the guard should be between 34 and 38 inches tall, measured from a line connecting the stair treads. If the handrail is mounted on the side of the stair guard, the guard should be at least 36 inches tall, and the handrail should be located between 34 and 38 inches above the line connecting the tread nosings. Refer to Figure 53.

4: Guards and Handrails   55

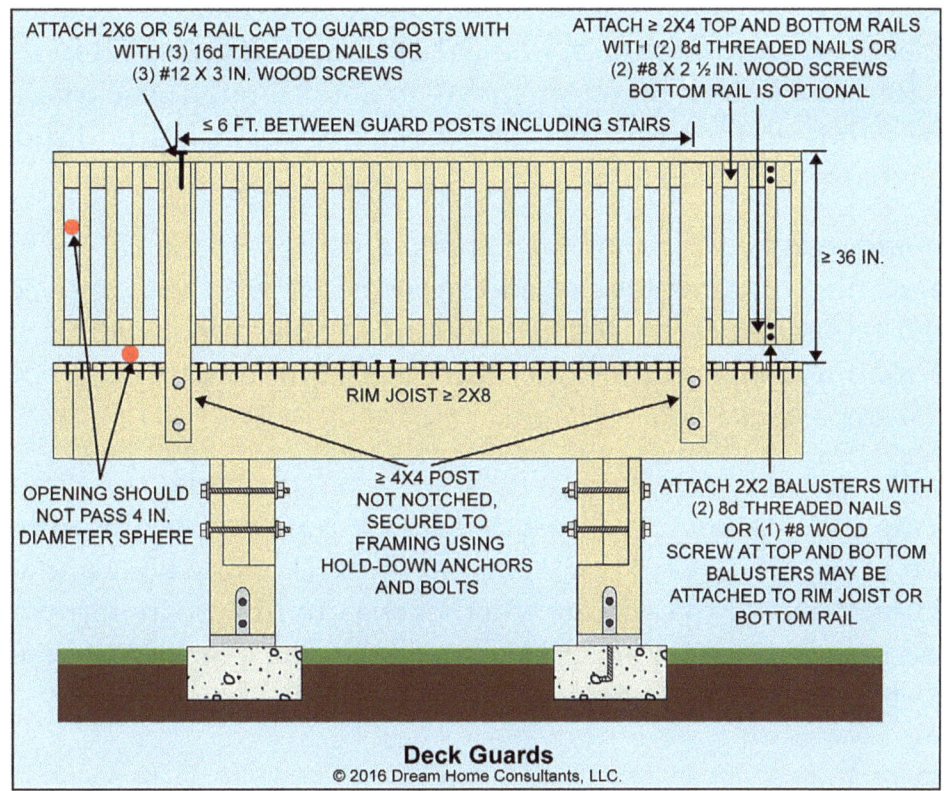

Figure 52

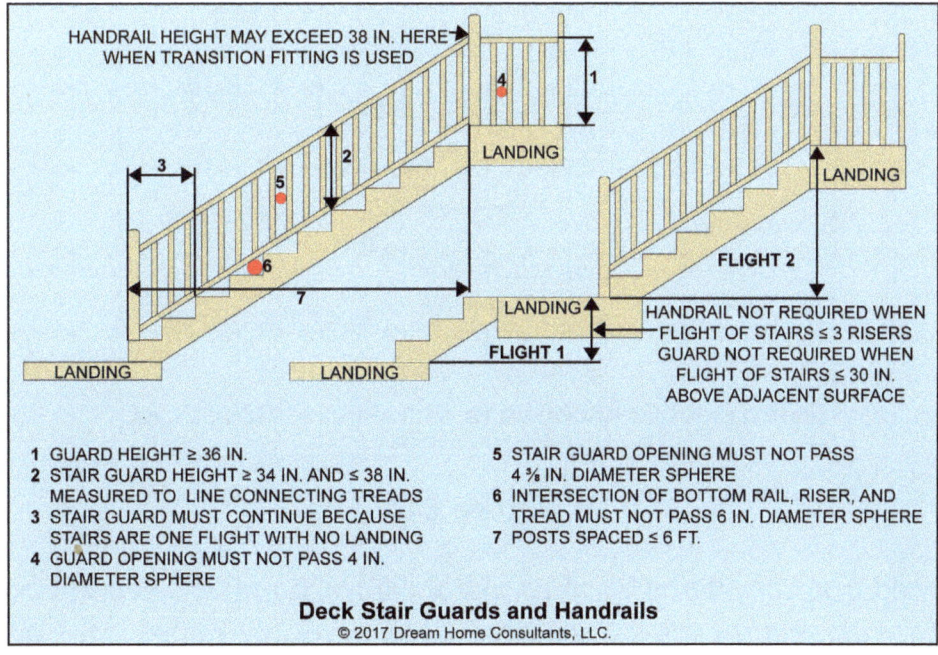

Figure 53

Openings between horizontal guard fill-in components should not allow a 4-inch diameter sphere to pass through. Openings between stair guard fill-in components should not allow a 4 ⅜-inch diameter sphere to pass through. The triangle formed between the stair riser, the tread, and the bottom rail of a stair guard should not allow a 6-inch diameter sphere to pass through. Refer to Figure 53.

A guard should resist a 200-pound load applied in any direction at the top without failing. Guard fill-in components should resist a 50-pound load applied horizontally without failing. Note that testing a guard to determine whether it complies with these requirements requires measurement equipment that is not available when evaluating a deck.

Pushing on the guard to determine if it moves when pushed is not a valid test, but it can indicate that the guard may be deficient if it moves significantly. A visual examination of how the guard is attached to the deck using bolts and connectors is the only practical way to estimate whether the guard system may comply with the IRC load requirements. Refer to Figure 54 for one example of how to attach guard posts to a deck. There are many other methods.

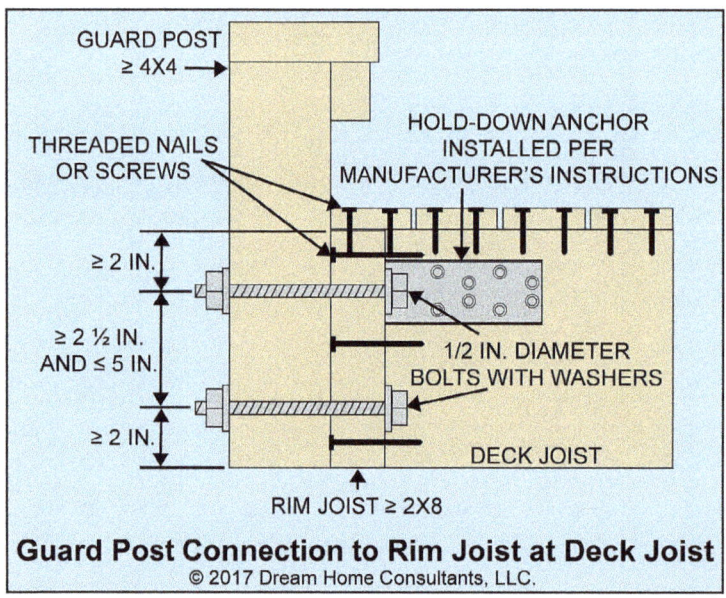

Figure 54

Manufactured guard systems, such as metal cables, metal fill-in components, and metal posts with metal cable or glazing fill-in components, should be installed according to manufacturer's instructions. These systems should have been independently tested to confirm compliance with IRC load requirements.

A handrail is required at a stairway with four or more risers. This includes the risers to the first and last treads, and to the landings. The handrail should be continuous from above the first riser to above the last riser. The handrail should terminate with a return, or at a post.

A handrail should be graspable. The IRC provides specific dimensions for handrail grip sizes. Most dimensional lumber used for deck handrails does not comply with the IRC handrail grip size requirements. Refer to Figure 55.

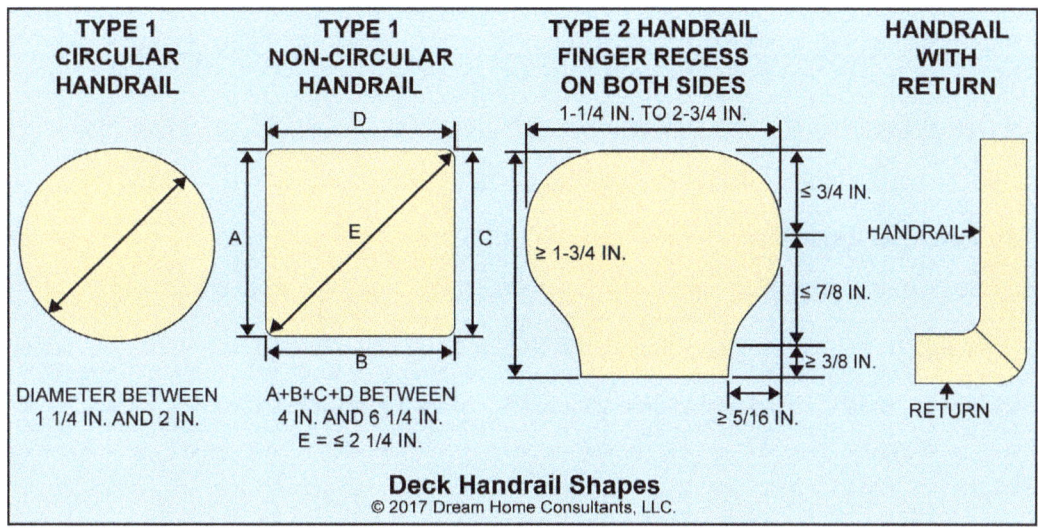

Figure 55

HISTORY

The general IRC guard and handrail requirements for decks are the same as those for interior guards and handrails. These requirements are found in IRC 2018 Table R301.5 (loads), and in Sections R311.7.8 (handrails) and R312.1 (guards). All editions of DCA 6 reference the general IRC guard and handrail requirements.

The general guard and handrail requirements have changed over time. The general IRC guard and handrail requirements have changed since the 2000 edition. The most significant changes include the 4 ⅜-inch opening size exception for stair guard fill-in components, which was added in 2006, and the 36-inch horizontal measurement requirement for determining whether a walking surface is more than 30 inches above grade, which was added in 2009. The most significant and common difference between the legacy codes and the IRC is that the legacy codes allowed a 6-inch sphere opening size for guard fill-in components. This affects decks built during the 1980s and 1990s.

The IRC does not provide details about how to install deck guards to comply with the load-resistance requirements. This allows for a wide variety of interpretations about how to comply. All editions of DCA 6 provide recommended installation details for installing a preservative-treated wood post and vertical baluster system that have been tested and demonstrated to comply with the IRC load requirements. These details have not changed significantly over the years.

4.1 - DEFECT – GUARD POST INSTALLATION DEFECTS

This category includes several common guard post defects, such as:

- no guard posts (Refer to Figure 56.);
- posts smaller than 4 x 4 (Refer to Figure 57.);
- notched posts of any size (Refer to Figure 58.);
- posts spaced more than 6 feet apart (Refer to Figures 59 and 60.);
- posts secured with only nails or screws (Refer to Figures 58, 61, and 64.);
- post attched using bolts smaller than ½-inch diameter;
- carriage bolts installed instead of machine bolts; fasteners counter-sunk or otherwise damage the post (Refer to Figure 68.);
- post bolts do not have washers on both ends, and a fully-threaded nut on the thread end (Refer to Figures 62 and 67.);
- posts attached to a stair stringer, or near other components that may not withstand the twisting load imposed by the guard (Refer to Figures 65 and 66.); and
- posts attached to deck framing members that are secured using only nails or screws (Refer to Figures 63 and 64.).

These guard post defects increase the risk of a guard failure. The reasons include:

- a guard secured only by balusters, guard posts that are smaller than 4 x 4, and guard posts that are spaced more than 6 feet apart may fail under a 200-pound load, especially as the wood and fasteners deteriorate with age;
- notched guard posts may split at the notch and fail under load;
- nails and screws that secure guards are likely to withdraw from the wood and fail under load, especially if fastened into the end grain of lumber, and especially as the wood and fasteners deteriorate with age; and

4: Guards and Handrails 59

- guards secured to framing members, such as rim joists and stringers, that are secured using nails or screws may fail because the framing member fasteners withdraw from the framing member causing the guard to fail.

Guard post installation defects create an unsafe condition. Action to correct these defects should be recommended. The safety concern is increased for older decks where the wood and the fasteners usually have deteriorated with age, even if the they do not present significant visible deterioration. The safety concern is also increased where multiple defects are present in the guard system.

Repair methods depend on the situation. Repair may be as simple as installing bolts and connectors, or as complex as installing a new guard system.

Figure 56

This guard has no posts, and is unlikely to comply with the 200-pound load requirement.

Figure 57

These guard posts are smaller than a 4 x 4, and are unlikely to comply with the 200-pound load requirement, no matter how they are attached to the deck. The wire fill-in component in the picture on the right does not comply with the fill-in component 50-pound load requirement.

Figure 58

The guard post on the left is both notched and is secured only with nails. Nail, screw or bolt attachment of a notched guard post is not allowed. Neither example is likely to comply with the 200-pound load requirement.

4: Guards and Handrails 61

Figure 59

Guard post spacing for both horizontal guard posts and stair guard posts is not more than every 6 feet. This stair guard does not comply.

Figure 60

Stair guard post support distance is measured horizontally as shown by the red lines. It is not measured along the length of the stair guard.

Figure 61

Guard posts should not be attached using screws, especially small screws like the post on the left. Even large screws are unlikely to comply with the 200-pound load requirement, especially when fastened into the end grain of lumber.

Figure 62

The bolts should be long enough to allow attachment of a washer and a nut.

4: Guards and Handrails

Figure 63

This guard post is attached to a rim joist that is secured only by nails or screws driven into the end grain of the joists. The bolts secure the post to the rim joist, but the screws or nails are likely to fail, allowing the guard to fail.

Figure 64

These pictures show what can happen when a guard is secured to a rim joist that is fastened using nails driven into the end grain of the deck floor joists. The rim joist detaches from the deck floor joists, then the guard detaches with the rim joist.

4: Guards and Handrails

Figure 65

Joist hangers, angle brackets, and similar connectors may fail under the twisting loads imposed by the deck posts.

Figure 66

A stair stringer is rarely secured well enough to withstand the twisting load imposed by a guard post, especially when the stringer is secured to the deck using only an uplift connector. This is an unsafe situation.

Figure 67

They probably did not have long enough bolts on the truck, so they notched the guard post and got just enough threads so that the nut would stay in place. This installation is unlikely to comply with the 200-pound load requirement.

Figure 68

Do not counter sink fasteners, as on the left, and do not use carriage bolts, as on the right. Both damage the wood so that the guard may not comply with the 200-pound load requirement.

4.2 - DEFECT – GUARD INSTALLATION DEFECTS

This category includes several common defects:

- guard not present at decks and stairs more than 30 inches above a surface (Refer to Figure 69.);
- guard less than 36 inches tall (42 inches where required by local building code) (Refer to Figure 70.); and
- stair guard with a handrail on top less than 34 inches or more than 38 inches tall (Refer to Figure 81.).

Guard installation defects create an unsafe condition. The primary reason is the increased risk of injury caused by falling. Action to correct these defects should be recommended.

Repair methods depend on the situation. These guard defects may require installation of a new guard system.

Figure 69

This porch is less than 30 inches above the mulch when measured straight down. When you measure 36 inches horizontally from the porch, then measure down, the porch is more than 30 inches above the mulch. A guard is required here, and would be required if this were a deck.

Figure 70

A bench may not substitute for a guard. It is okay to have a bench in front of an approved guard.

4.3 - DEFECT – GUARD FILL-IN COMPONENT INSTALLATION DEFECTS

This category includes several common defects:

- horizontal guard openings allow a 4-inch diameter sphere to pass through, including between vertical fill-in components and under any guard bottom rail (Refer to Figures 71, 73, 74, and 75.);
- stair guard openings allow a 4 ⅜-inch diameter sphere to pass through;
- triangle formed by the stair riser, tread, and any guard bottom rail allows passage of a 6-inch diameter sphere (Refer to Figure 72.);
- lattice or other fill-in component material that may not comply with the 50-pound load requirement (Refer to Figure 76.);
- wood balusters attached with one nail (Refer to Figure 77.);
- loose metal cable fill-in components (Refer to Figure 78.);
- insect screens used in place of fill-in components (Refer to Figure 71.); and
- glazing in guards not safety glazing.

Guard fill-in component installation defects may create an unsafe condition. The primary reasons are the increased risk of strangulation of children who get their head stuck between the components, and the increased risk of children falling between the fill-in components.

The recommendation to address these defects depends on the situation. Action should be recommended to correct fill-in component openings that allow passage of a greater than 6-inch diameter sphere, wood balusters attached with one nail, lack of safety glazing, and loose metal cable fill-in components.

Action should be recommended to correct fill-in component openings that allow passage of a greater than 4-inch diameter sphere for decks built after about 2000. Fill-in component openings that allow passage of a sphere between 4 and 6 inches in diameter for decks built before about 2000 should, at least, be reported and the risk should be explained.

Repair methods depend on the situation.

Figure 71

Insect screens may not substitute for guard fill-in components.

4: Guards and Handrails

Figure 72

The area below a stair guard bottom rail should not allow a 6-inch diameter sphere to pass through.

Figure 73

The space under a guard should not allow a 4-inch diameter sphere to pass through.

4: Guards and Handrails

Figure 74

Fill-in components of older deck guards may allow a 6-inch diameter sphere to pass through. This is often considered acceptable for older decks, although this does not comply with current IRC requirements.

Figure 75

Fill-in components with decorative designs may not comply with the 4-inch diameter sphere requirement. While not prohibited by the IRC, fill-in components that can be climbed may be an issue for families with children.

4: Guards and Handrails 71

Figure 76

Lattice may or may not comply with the 50-pound load requirement.

Figure 77

Wood balusters should be fastened either with two nails or one screw.

4: Guards and Handrails

Figure 78

When metal cables are used as guard fill-in components, it should not be easy to move them so that a 4-inch diameter sphere may pass through.

4.4 - DEFECT – HANDRAIL INSTALLATION DEFECTS

This category includes several common defects:

- handrail not present at stairs with four or more risers (Refer to Figure 79.),
- handrail grip not approved dimensions (including dimensional lumber handrails other than a 2 x 2) (Refer to Figure 80.),
- handrail less than 34 inches or more than 38 inches above the treads (Refer to Figure 81.),
- handrail not continuous from above the top riser to above the bottom riser (Refer to Figure 82.), and
- handrail does not terminate with a return or a post (Refer to Figure 80.).

Handrail installation defects create an unsafe condition. The primary reason is the increased risk of injury caused by falling. Action to correct these defects should be recommended.

4: Guards and Handrails 73

Repair methods depend on the situation. A building code-compliant handrail can often be added to the side of a stair guard. This does not include installing a preservative-treated 2 x 2 along the side of the stair guard, unless the supports are spaced very close together. A 2 x 2 may break under a horizontal (lateral) load.

Figure 79

There are four risers, so there should be a handrail on at least one side. There should be a guard on both sides of this flight of stairs if the top landing is more than 30 inches above the ground.

74   4: Guards and Handrails

Figure 80

This handrail is not graspable, and does not terminate in a return. Also note that the space between treads is too large and would allow a 4-inch diameter sphere to pass through.

Figure 81

This stair guard and handrail is less than 34 inches tall, thus is too low.

Figure 82

This handrail stops before the leading edge of the bottom riser, thus it does not comply with the continuous handrail requirement. It is also not graspable (Refer to Figure 55.).

4.5 - DEFECT – DECK COMPONENTS PENETRATE WALL COVERINGS

Deck components should not penetrate wall coverings, or be attached through wall coverings. Guards are the most common deck components that penetrate wall coverings, although framing members such as floor joists occasionally do so. The primary reason for this is that wall covering penetrations are difficult to flash, and because sealants that are frequently used to fill the gaps around penetrations require maintenance to keep the sealants from allowing water infiltration.

The deck ledger board is not considered a penetration for purposes of this defect because removal of wall coverings is required, and because deck ledger board should be properly flashed. Cantilevered floor joists are not considered a penetration form purposes of this defect. Determining their condition is out-of-scope of a deck evaluation because their condition where they penetrate the wall covering cannot be evaluated visually.

Deck components that penetrate wall coverings do not create an unsafe condition. Evaluation of the situation should be recommended. Closer inspection of the visible areas around and under the penetration, both inside and outside the building, is prudent. Repair methods depend on the situation.

4.6 - DEFECT – DETERIORATED, DAMAGED, AND LOOSE GUARDS, HANDRAILS, AND HARDWARE

This category includes several common defects. Refer to the discussions about wood and hardware deterioration in the Deck Ledger Attachment to the Building chapter for additional discussion about deteriorated wood and hardware. These defects include:

- visibly deteriorated (rotted), and visibly damaged wood (Refer to Figure 83.),
- hardware presenting significant red rust, and
- guard or handrail moves significantly when pushed or pulled.

Note that a guard or handrail that does not move when pushed or pulled is not necessarily building code-compliant or safe. If, however, the guard or handrail moves significantly when pushed or pulled, it probably is not building code-compliant, and is probably unsafe.

Visibly deteriorated and significantly loose handrails and guards create an unsafe condition. The primary reason is the increased risk of injury caused by falling. Action to correct these defects should be recommended. Repair methods depend on the situation.

Deteriorated and loose guards and handrails are often found on older decks where several components may be near the end of their service life. It may be more cost-effective to replace the defective guards, handrails, and related components rather than trying to repair them.

Figure 83 courtesy of Randy Sipe

This guard system is significantly deteriorated, and is likely to fail.

5: STAIRWAYS AND LANDINGS

OVERVIEW

Decks are not required to have stairways, although many decks have them. Stairways provide access between the deck and the ground, or between two or more areas of the deck that are at different elevations.

A stairway and landing may be built like a deck in order to provide access to an exterior door. A stairway to an exterior door may serve as a way to enter and leave the building in an emergency, and if so the stairway is called a means of egress. A stairway serving the front door to a building usually serves the required means of egress door. It is important that means of egress stairways, especially the stairway serving the front door, comply with all building code and best practice requirements.

Stairways are inherently dangerous. Stairways should be safe to use for all who might be expected to use them. This includes children and those with reduced mobility.

Deck stairways are subject to rain, snow, and other environmental conditions, and may have longer unsupported runs compared to interior stairs. Stair stringer attachment to the deck, stair stringer span distance, and stair stringer support are especially important for deck stairs.

IMPLICATIONS OF DECK STAIRWAY FAILURE

Falls while using deck stairways are one of the most common types of deck-related injuries. Deck stairway collapse, while less common than falls, is also a risk. Because falls and stairway collapses can result in fatalities, injury, and property damage, improper stairway installation, and deteriorated stairways, are often unsafe conditions.

GENERAL STAIRWAY AND LANDING REQUIREMENTS

Stairways should be at least 36 inches wide, measured above the handrail. When the handrail is mounted on top of the stair guard, which it usually is for decks, the stairway should be at least 36 inches wide between the stair guards.

Stairway risers (the vertical part) should be not more than 7 ¾ inches tall, including at the top and bottom landings. Measurement is between the leading edges of adjacent treads. The riser height difference between any two risers in a flight of stairs should not be more than ⅜ inch. Openings between treads should be filled so that a 4-inch diameter sphere will not pass through.

Stairway treads (the horizontal part) should be at least 10 inches deep plus a nosing, or at least 11 inches deep without a nosing. Measurement is between the leading edges of adjacent treads. The tread depth difference between any two treads in a flight of stairs should not be more than ⅜ inch.

A nosing is an extension of a tread or a landing above the riser below. A nosing is not required. The minimum nosing depth is ¾ inch, and the maximum depth is 1 ¼ inches, if a nosing is installed. The nosing depth difference between treads in a stairway should not be more than ⅜ inch. A nosing is not required if the tread depth is at least 11 inches.

Figure 84 shows the nosing dimensions and profiles based on the IRC requirements. While the nosing profiles are, technically, required for deck stairways as they are for interior stairways, most inspectors do not make an issue about nosing profiles if the minimum and maximum nosing depths comply with the IRC.

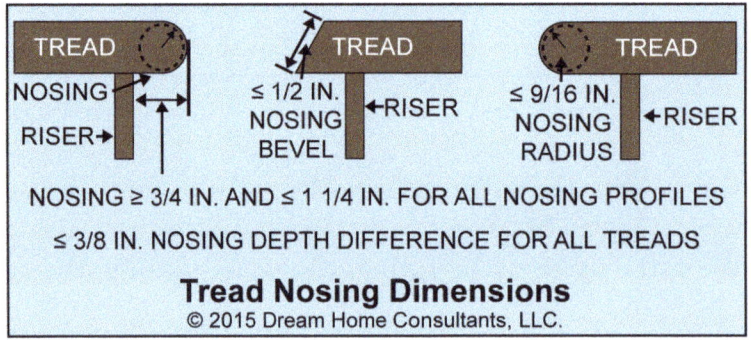

Figure 84

5: Stairways and Landings 81

Most stairway treads are rectangular. A winder tread is a tread with a triangle-like shape that is used to change the direction of the stairway. Spiral stairways are those that have treads attached to a center post and rise in a spiral shape. Winder treads and spiral stairways are less common deck stairways. The requirements for these deck stairways are the same as those for interior stairways. Refer to Figures 85 and 86.

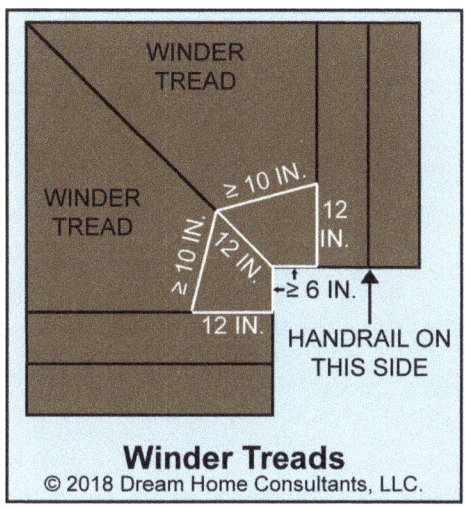

Figure 85

The illustration on the top shows the required minimum dimensions of a winder tread. The winder tread dimensions in the picture below the illustration are way too small.

82   5: Stairways and Landings

Figure 86

This is a picture of a spiral stairway serving a deck.

A solid landing should be installed at the top and at the bottom of a flight of stairs. The landing should be at least as wide as the stairway, and at least 36 inches deep in the direction of travel. A flight of stairs should not rise vertically more than 151 inches (IRC 2018 R 311.7.3) without being interrupted by a landing.

DCA 6 provides best practice details for installing a deck stairway. Stringers should be supported at the deck by a stringer hanger, but this practice is not often followed. Nails and screws can work as stringer support at the deck if properly installed, and if the stringers are restrained against horizontal (lateral) movement. Stringers should be supported at the bottom landing by a wood block and the post supported on a footing, but this practice is not often followed. Alternate stringer support methods can work if the stringers are supported by at least 1 ½ inches of wood at the heel of the bottom stringer cut. Refer to Figure 87.

5: Stairways and Landings

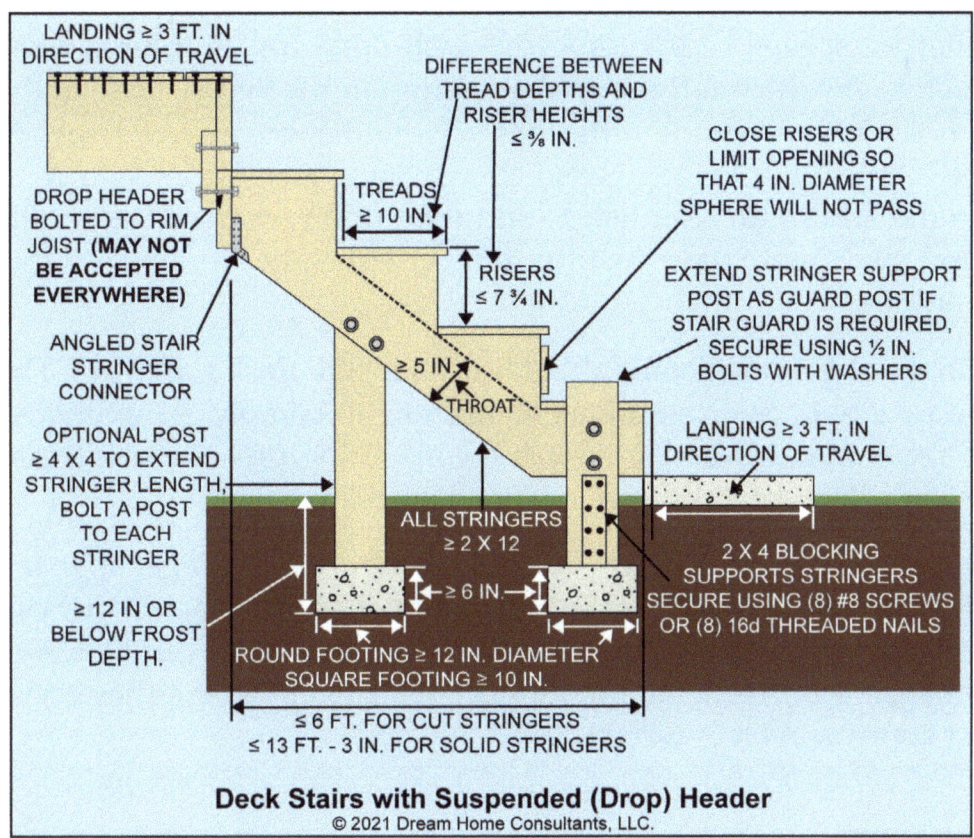

Figure 87

HISTORY

The general IRC deck stairway requirements are the same as those for **interior** stairways. These requirements are found in IRC 2018 Table R301.5 (loads), and in Sections R311.5 and R311.7. All editions of DCA 6 reference the general IRC stairway requirements, and include additional details about deck stairway construction best practices.

Stairway requirements have changed over time, including requirements in the legacy codes (codes before the IRC), and in the IRC. The IRC stairway requirements have changed since the 2000 edition. For example, the requirement to fill the space between open risers first appeared in the 2012 edition. These changes, however, do not affect the requirements for existing deck stairways.

The most significant and common differences between the legacy codes and the IRC are that the legacy codes allowed 9-inch deep treads (plus a nosing), and either 8-inch or 8 ¼-inch tall risers, depending on the legacy code and the year. This affects decks built through the 1990s. Note that maximum riser height and tread depth limits vary among jurisdictions. Some jurisdictions currently allow more than the minimum riser height and the minimum tread depth allowed by the IRC, and allow more than the minimum riser height difference at the top and bottom landings.

The IRC does not provide details about how to install deck stairways. This allows for a wide variety of interpretations about how to comply. All editions of DCA 6 provide recommended best practices for installing preservative-treated wood deck stairways. These details have changed over time.

One significant change is a reduction in the unsupported stringer span from 7-feet to 6-feet for cut stringers, and from 16-feet, 6-inches to 13-feet, 3-inches for solid stringers. Refer to Figure 87. This change first appears in a 2013 DCA 6 update. Another change is in the detail for support of stringers where they end at grade, which first appears in DCA 6-2009.

5.1 - DEFECT – IMPROPER RISER HEIGHT, TREAD DEPTH, AND NOSING DEPTH

A riser height that is greater than allowed, a tread depth that is less than allowed, or a nosing depth that is greater than allowed, increase the risk of falling while using the stairway. The primary risk is to children, and to those with impaired mobility; however, all stairway users are at some risk, especially in cases where there are small treads and deep nosings. Refer to Figures 84, 85, 87, and 88.

A riser height that is more than currently allowed, a tread depth that is less than currently allowed, or a nosing depth that is greater than allowed, may create an unsafe condition; however, it is not necessary to recommend evaluation or repair of these conditions if the risers, treads, and nosings conform to current local building code, or if they may have conformed to local legacy codes when the stairway was built.

Action to correct these defects should be recommended if the previous exception does not apply. Action should be recommended to correct riser height greater than 8 ¼ inches, tread depth less than 9 inches, and nosing depth greater than 1 ¼ inch. Proper repair of this defect may require replacing the stairway.

Figure 88

The extension of the flooring over this tread creates a nosing that is too deep, thus is a trip and fall hazard.

5.2 - DEFECT – IMPROPER RISER HEIGHT, TREAD DEPTH, AND NOSING DEPTH DIFFERENCES

A riser height difference, or a tread or a nosing depth difference, that is more than ⅜ inch increases the risk of falling while using the stairway. All stairway users are at risk because any person using the stairway becomes accustomed to the risers, treads, and nosings, and may trip and fall if the riser height, or the tread or the nosing depth change. Refer to Figure 89.

Riser height or tread and nosing depth differences that are more than ⅜ inch create an unsafe condition. Action to correct these defects should be recommended. Note, however, that some jurisdictions allow a greater riser height difference at top and bottom landings.

Proper repair of riser height differences may require replacing the stairway. Repair of tread and nosing depth differences can sometimes be accomplished by replacing some or all treads. Replacing only some treads may create a defect (nosing depth difference).

Figure 89

The top riser height (short) is quite different from the middle two risers, and the bottom riser height (tall) is quite different from the other risers. Although there are only four risers, these stairs are unsafe.

5.3 - DEFECT – RISER OPENING BETWEEN TREADS ALLOWS 4-INCH DIAMETER SPHERE TO PASS

A riser opening between treads that allows passage of a 4-inch diameter sphere creates an unsafe condition. Refer to Figure 90. The primary reasons are the increased risk of strangulation of children who get their head stuck between the components, and the increased risk of children falling between the treads. Action should be recommended to fill in the riser opening. Note that filling riser openings that are less than 30 inches above the surface below is not required.

Repair can usually be accomplished by installing a piece of wood to close the opening.

Figure 90

The space between these treads should be filled so that a 4-inch diameter sphere cannot pass through. Given the amount of deterioration, it may be prudent to replace this stairway.

5.4 - DEFECT – INADEQUATE STRINGER SUPPORT AT DECK OR TOP OF LANDING

DCA 6 recommends attaching deck stairway stringers at the deck or the landing using a stringer hanger designed for this purpose, such as the Simpson model LSC. This is the best attachment method, but this practice is not often followed.

Most deck stair stringers are attached using nails, and occasionally using screws. Stringers attached using only nails and screws are prone to failure. There are several ways these stringers can fail including: (1) stringer detaching from support, (2) stringer fasteners withdrawing from support, (3) stringer splitting along the wood grain. Attachment using nails or screws can work if:

- the stringers are securely restrained against lateral (horizontal) movement (Refer to Figures 93 and 94.), and if
- the entire plumb (vertical) cut of the stringer bears on the deck or landing (Refer to Figures 91 and 92.), and if
- enough nails or screws of sufficient thickness and length are installed (Refer to Figure 92.), and if

- the rim joist to which the stringers are attached is well-supported, and is deep enough so that it will not deflect when the stairway is used (Refer to Figure 95.), and if
- there is no visible evidence of wood or fastener damage or deterioration at the stringer, and at the attachment point to the deck or landing.

Figure 91

The entire stringer plumb cut should bear on the support. If it does not, the stringers may detach from the support, or they may split along the wood grain.

Figure 92

Even if the entire stringer plumb cut bears on support, enough fasteners must be installed to secure the stringer to the support. There are not enough visible fasteners in either picture. The wood under the stringer in the picture on the right does not provide useful support for the stringer.

Figure 93

Sometimes the stringer will pull away from the fasteners if the stringer is not restrained against lateral movement. The strap does not help much.

Figure 94

Sometimes the fasteners will withdraw from support, especially when the wood is deteriorated from years of exposure to moisture.

Figure 95

These stringers are supported using a drop header that is fastened using only nails. Also note that the rim joist that supports the drop header is supported by an angle bracket. Both are defects, making this an unsafe stairway.

Inadequate attachment of deck stairway stringers to the deck or landing increases the risk of stairway collapse. The primary reason is that fasteners withdraw from the stringers or that the stringers withdraw from the deck or landing.

Inadequate attachment of deck stairway stringers to a deck or to a landing may create an unsafe condition. Evaluation of the stringers and their attachment to the deck should be recommended.

Repair of this defect depends on the situation. Providing stringer support near the center of the stringer as described in DCA 6, or by another reasonable method, may be a comparatively inexpensive option. This is for stairways that are not damaged or deteriorated, and that appear to be within their service life.

5.5 - DEFECT – IMPROPER DROP HEADER INSTALLATION

DCA 6 recommends attaching deck stairway stringers directly to the deck, or to the landing. Deck builders often prefer to use the deck or landing rim joist as the last riser in the flight of stairs because it makes installing the guard and handrail easier. Using the rim joist as the last riser makes it difficult to have the stringer plumb cut fully bearing on the rim joist. Some deck builders attempt to solve this problem using a drop header.

Neither the IRC nor DCA 6 provide details about how to install a drop header. A drop header secured to the rim joist only by nails or screws is not acceptable. Refer to Figures 96 and 97. A drop header that is secured to the rim joist using galvanized steel or stainless steel machine bolts with washers on both ends may be acceptable. There is no authoritative source for the bolt size, but at least ⅜ inch diameter, or larger, bolts are sometimes used. Bolts should be installed near the center of the wood used to connect the deck rim joist to the drop header, and should be installed at least two inches (preferably more) from the edges of the deck rim joist and the drop header. Refer to Figure 98.

Attachment of a drop header using only nails or screws increases the risk of stairway collapse. The primary reason is that fasteners withdraw from the drop header or from the rim joist.

Attachment of a drop header using only nails or screws creates an unsafe condition. Action to correct this defect should be recommended.

Repair of this defect is usually accomplished by installing bolts to secure the drop header to the rim joist.

Figure 96

This attempt at a drop header (the three 2 x 4s) is secured only by nails that may work loose over time and cause a stairway collapse. Also, look closely at the upper left corner of the picture. The rim joist is supported by an angle bracket. This is another defect.

Figure 97

This drop header is also secured only by nails that may work loose over time and cause a stairway collapse. Also, the riser openings need to be closed so that a 4-inch diameter sphere will not pass through.

Figure 98

Bolts that attach a drop header should be installed in the center one third of the wood to avoid splitting the wood. Both bolts in the picture on the left are too close to the edge of the vertical member. The lower bolt is also too close to the top of the drop header. All of the bolts in the picture on the right are too close to the edge of the vertical members.

5.6 - DEFECT – IMPROPER STRINGER SUPPORT AT THE BOTTOM OF THE STAIRWAY

DCA 6 recommends supporting the bottom of a stringer using a 4 x 4 post, a 2 x 4 bearing block, and a footing. This is a good support method, but it is uncommon because of the labor and material costs. Many deck stairway stringers are supported on a landing, or by some other method. Additional methods of supporting stringers at the bottom of the flight of stairs can be acceptable if:

- the stringers are securely restrained against lateral (horizontal) movement, and if
- at least 1 ½ inches of the heel (rear end) of the seat (horizontal) cut of the stringer bears on the support (Refer to Figure 99.), and if
- the bottom of the support is below the frost depth, and if
- there is no visible evidence of wood damage or deterioration at the stringer and at the support.

Inadequate support of deck stairway stringers at the bottom of the stairway increases the risk of stairway collapse. The primary reason is that the stringers can split or deteriorate, causing them to deform and place an increased load on the attachment point at the top of the flight of stairs. This increased load can, in turn, cause the stringers to withdraw from the attachment point and collapse.

Inadequate support of deck stairway stringers at the bottom of the stairway may create an unsafe condition. Evaluation of the situation should be recommended.

Repair of this defect depends on the situation. Providing stringer support near the center of the stringer as described in DCA 6, or by another reasonable method, may be a comparatively inexpensive option for stairways that are not damaged or deteriorated, and that appear to be within their service life.

Figure 99-1

This stringer bears on a small area of the toe (front edge). The stringer may split along the wood grain and fail causing a stairway collapse.

Figure 99-2

This stringer also bears on a small area of the toe (front edge). The stringer is further weakened by the saw over-cut (saw kerf).

5.7 - DEFECT – STRINGER INSTALLATION DEFECTS

These defects are among the most common, and are based on not complying with DCA 6 recommendations:

- stringer not at least a 2 x 12,
- stringer throat depth less than 5 inches deep (Refer to Figure 100.),
- unsupported cut stringer span more than 6 feet (Refer to Figure 101.), and
- unsupported solid stringer span more than 13 feet, 3 inches.

Stringers are sometimes constructed using 2 x 10s, especially stringers for older decks. This can be acceptable if the unsupported span does not exceed the current recommended distance, and if the stringer throat depth is not less than the current recommended depth. Note that some jurisdictions allow a stringer throat depth less than 5 inches.

Stringer installation defects create an unsafe condition. The primary reason is that the stringers may split, or that they may deflect under load in such a way that they place too much load on the stringer support at the deck or at the landing. Refer to Figure 91. Both conditions can cause the stairway to collapse. Action to correct these defects should be recommended. Note, however, that some jurisdictions allow different stringer installation details.

Repair methods depend on the situation. Providing stringer support near the center of the stringer as described in DCA 6, or by another reasonable method, may be a comparatively inexpensive option for stairways that are not damaged or deteriorated, and that appear to be within their service life.

Figure 100

Stringer throat depth is measured to the saw kerf (cut) as shown in the picture on the left, or to the triangle cut as shown in the picture on the right. These stringers do not have enough intact wood to support the load on the stairway.

Figure 101

These cut stringer spans are much longer than 6 feet. So are the spans between the guard posts.

5.8 - DEFECT – IMPROPER STRINGER INTERMEDIATE SUPPORT

DCA 6 recommends using a notched 4 x 4 post supported by a footing, and secured to the stringer using a ½-inch diameter bolt when providing intermediate support to a stringer between the top and the bottom of a flight of stairs. This is done to reduce the unsupported stringer span so that the stringer complies with the span distance requirement. This is a good support method, but it is uncommon because of the expense. Other methods of providing intermediate stringer support may be acceptable if:

- at least 1 ½ inches of the stringer bears on the support, and if
- the stringer is securely attached to the support in order to resist horizontal (lateral) movement, and if
- support posts are securely attached to the support footing, and if
- the bottom of the support footing is below the frost depth, and if
- there is no visible evidence of wood or hardware damage or deterioration at the stringer and at the intermediate support.

5: Stairways and Landings

Inadequate support of deck stairway stringers increases the risk of stairway collapse. Refer to Figure 102. The primary reason is that the stringers can split or deteriorate causing them to deform and place an increased load on the attachment point at the top of the flight of stairs. This increased load can, in turn, cause the stringers to withdraw from the attachment point and contribute to a stairway collapse.

Inadequate support of deck stairway stringers may create an unsafe condition. Evaluation of the situation should be recommended.

Repair of this defect depends on the situation. Providing stringer support near the center of the stringer as described in DCA 6, or by another reasonable method, may be a comparatively inexpensive option for stairways that are not damaged or deteriorated, and that appear to be within their service life.

Figure 102

This is an attempt to provide stringer intermediate support. It does not do much, if any, good.

5.9 - DEFECT – TREAD INSTALLATION DEFECTS

DCA 6 recommends that when using cut stringers, at least 3 stringers should be installed for a 36-inch wide stairway. More stringers are recommended if the stairway is wider. DCA 6 recommends using at least 2 x 4 or 5/4 x __ dimensional lumber for tread material, with a maximum unsupported tread span of 18 inches.

DCA 6 recommends that when using solid stringers, at least 2 stringers should be installed for a 36-inch wide stairway. More stringers are recommended if the stairway is wider. DCA 6 recommends using at least 2 x 8 treads for most common lumber species, with a maximum unsupported tread span of 36 inches. Refer to Figure 103.

Note that treads made from materials other than dimensional lumber should be installed according to manufacturer's instructions. These materials include wood composites (such as Trex), plastic, and metal. Allowed tread spans for these materials may be less than those for dimensional lumber. Allowed clearance between these materials and the ground may also be less than clearances for dimensional lumber.

Stringer and tread installations that do not comply with these recommendations create an unsafe condition. The primary reason is that the stringers or treads may deflect during use, or deform with use and age, and cause someone to lose balance and fall. Action to correct these defects should be recommended. Repair of tread material defects usually involves replacing the tread material. Repair of stringer defects may involve adding a stringer.

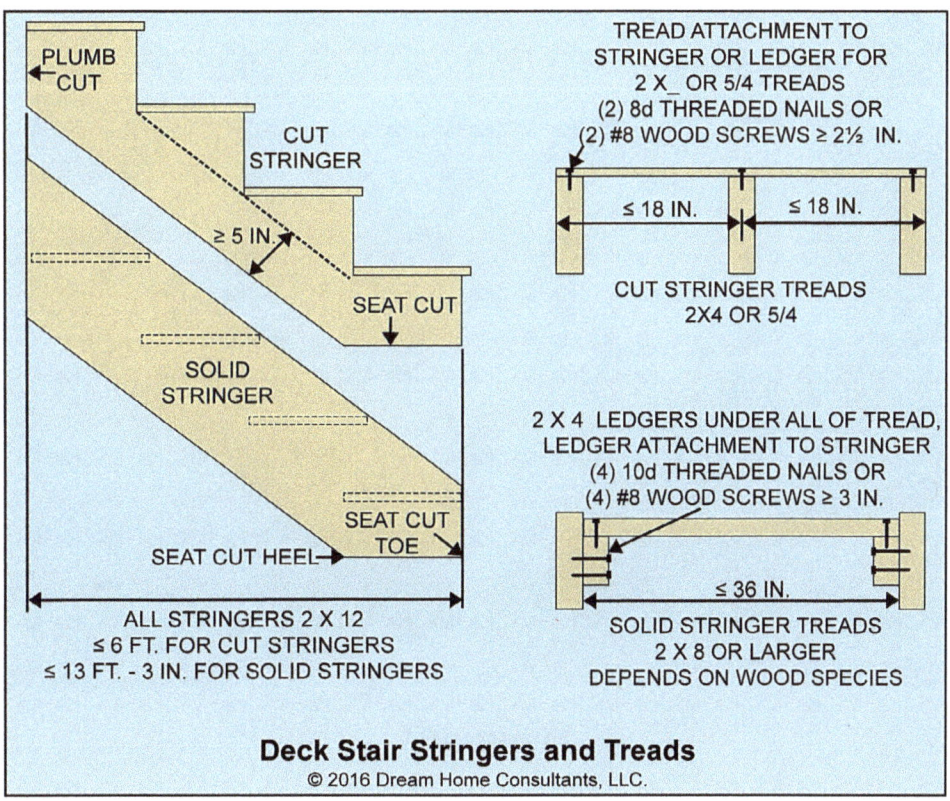

Figure 103

5.10 - DEFECT – LANDING DEFECTS

The IRC requires a landing at the top and at the bottom of every flight of stairs. Typical landing defects include: (1) lack of a landing at the top or at the bottom of a flight of stairs, (2) lack of an intermediate landing for stairways with a vertical rise of more than 151 inches, and (3) landings that are less than 36 inches deep in the direction of travel. All of these defects increase the risk of falling while using the stairway. All stairway users are at risk because these defects are a trip and fall hazard, and lack of an intermediate landing makes the stairway more difficult to use for children and for people with impaired mobility.

Landing defects create an unsafe condition. Action to correct these defects should be recommended. Note, however, that some jurisdictions do not require solid landings where the stairway terminates at grade.

Repair of landing defects depends on the situation.

Figure 104

Most jurisdictions do not consider soil to be an approved landing. A solid surface, such as concrete, is often required.

5.11 - DEFECT – DETERIORATED AND DAMAGED STAIR-WAYS AND HARDWARE

This defect category includes several common defects. Refer to the discussions about wood and hardware deterioration in the Deck Ledger Attachment to the Building chapter for additional discussion about deteriorated wood and hardware. These defects include:

- visibly deteriorated (rotted), and visibly damaged wood (Refer to Figure 105.);
- hardware presenting red rust; and
- stringers or treads deflect significantly when walked upon.

Deteriorated and damaged stairways and hardware create an unsafe condition. The primary reason is the increased risk of injury caused by falling. Action to correct these defects should be recommended.

Repair methods depend on the situation. Deteriorated and damaged stairways and hardware are often found on older decks. It may be more cost-effective to replace the stairway and related components rather than trying to repair them.

Figure 105

Even preservative-treated wood will eventually deteriorate, especially if cuts are not field-treated with a preservative.

6: DECK FRAMING

OVERVIEW

Deck framing should provide a structurally-stable and long-lasting deck for use by building occupants. For purposes of this book, deck framing includes:

- deck floor joists and rim joists,
- deck beams,
- deck bracing,
- deck flooring, and
- deck hardware (e.g., joist hangers, angle brackets, uplift connectors, and fasteners).

IMPLICATIONS OF DECK FRAMING FAILURE

Deck failures caused solely by one deck framing defect are uncommon. It is more likely that multiple deck framing defects combine with each other, or that they combine with other deck component defects. These defects include a deck ledger attachment defect, a deck stairway defect, or a deck guard defect, which contribute to a deck failure. A deck framing defect, by itself, is unlikely to cause an unsafe condition. Deck framing defects should, however, be reported when encountered, and action should be taken to address these defects.

GENERAL DECK FRAMING REQUIREMENTS

Wood used for most deck components should be preservative-treated wood that is rated for ground contact (UC4A or better), or should be naturally durable wood such as redwood and western cedar. Naturally durable wood is not rated for ground contact unless it is preservative-treated. Exceptions to the ground contact-rated rule include wood deck guard components (other than guard posts), and most wood deck flooring. Note that it is not possible to visually determine if wood is ground-contact rated unless the manufacturer's label is still attached to the wood. This is uncommon.

The length of deck floor joists and beams between supports (spans), and any extension of the deck floor joist beyond a supporting beam (a cantilever) should be based on the tables in the IRC, or on the tables in DCA 6. Number 2 grade or better lumber and wet service conditions are assumed in these tables. Do not use the tables for interior floor joists and beams when determining deck floor joist and deck beam spans. Note that the IRC and DCA 6 span tables contain different values. Refer to Figure 106 for an illustration that describes how to measure deck floor joist span and cantilever span.

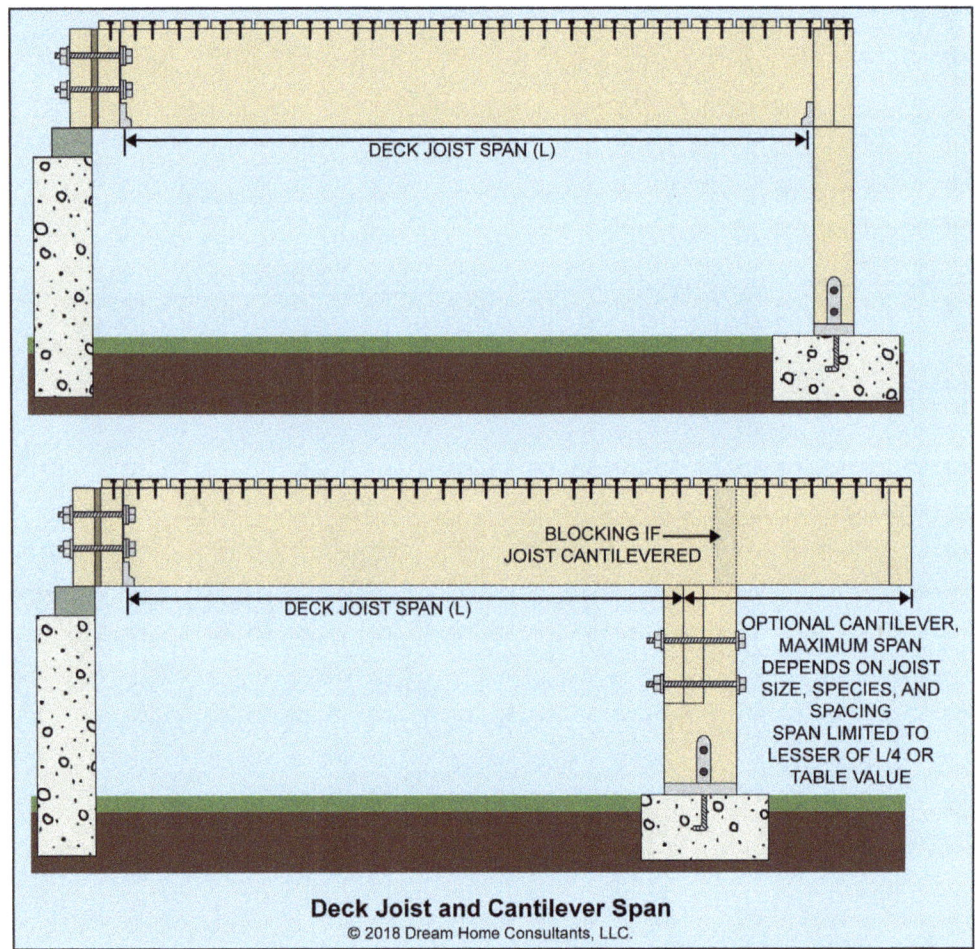

Figure 106

DCA 6 recommends that deck floor joists should bear on top of the beam, or that they should be supported by a joist hanger when they bear on the side of a beam. Deck floor joists should be supported by a joist hanger when they bear on the deck ledger board. The IRC added this requirement in 2018. Support of deck floor joists by a ledger strip (usually a 2 x 2) is not allowed by IRC 2018, or by DCA 6, but this support method was allowed in previous IRC editions. Refer to Figure 107.

6: Deck Framing 105

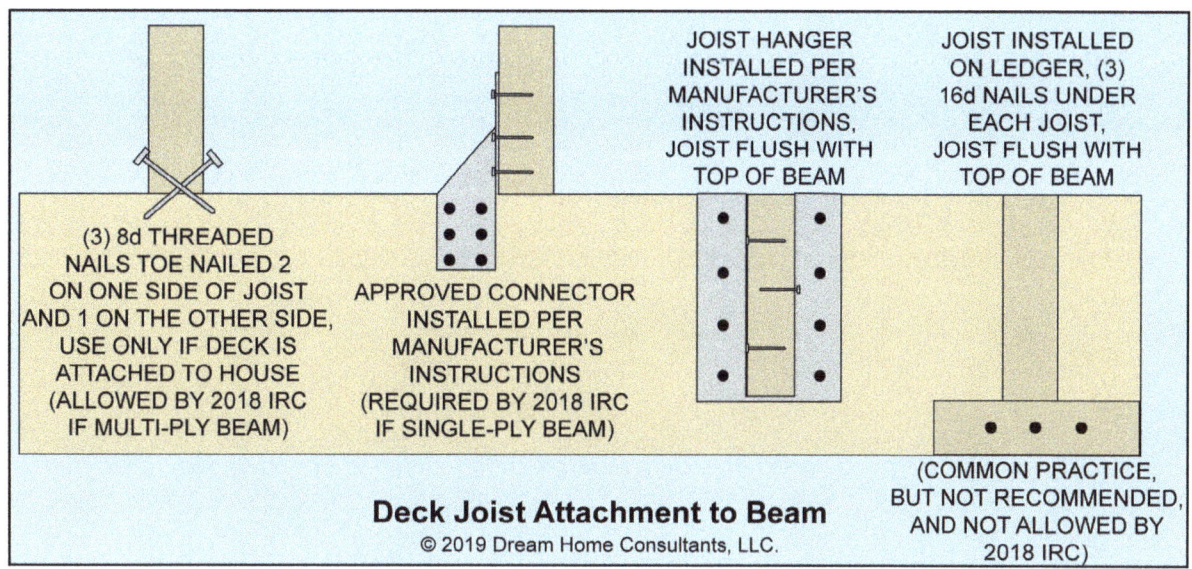

Figure 107

DCA 6 recommends that the rim joist at the end of the deck floor joists should be fastened to the floor joists and to the deck flooring using 10d threaded nails or #10 x 3-inch wood screws. The IRC did not specify rim joist attachment details until IRC 2018. Refer to Figure 108.

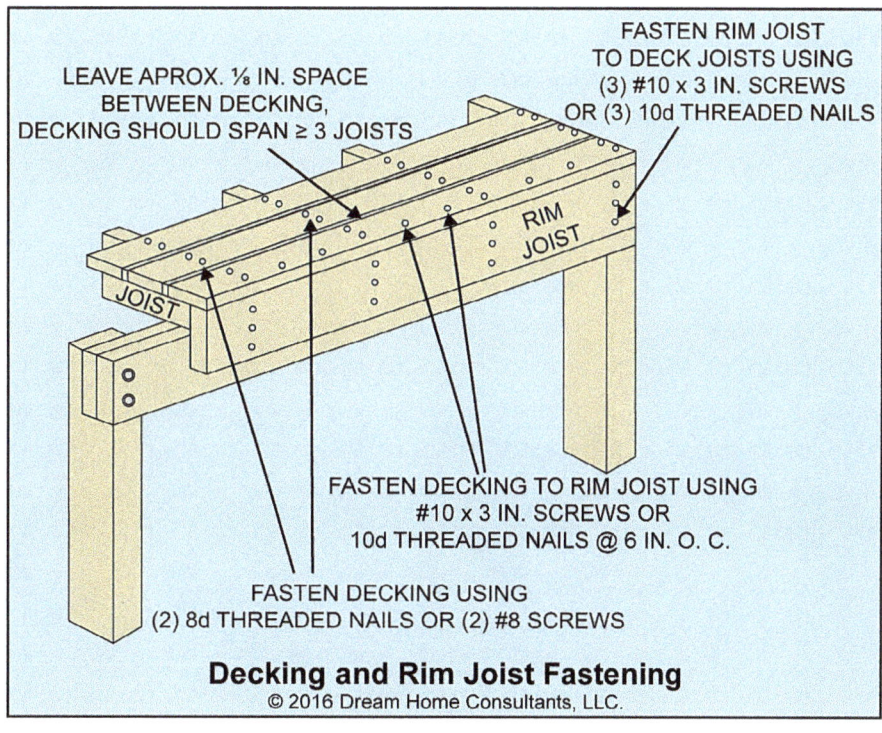

Figure 108

Deck beams are often made from two or three pieces of dimensional lumber that should be nailed or screwed together as recommended in DCA 6. Refer to Figure 109. The IRC allows single-member beams, but DCA 6 does not mention single-member beams. Glue-laminated deck beams and steel deck beams are allowed, but are beyond the scope of a deck evaluation.

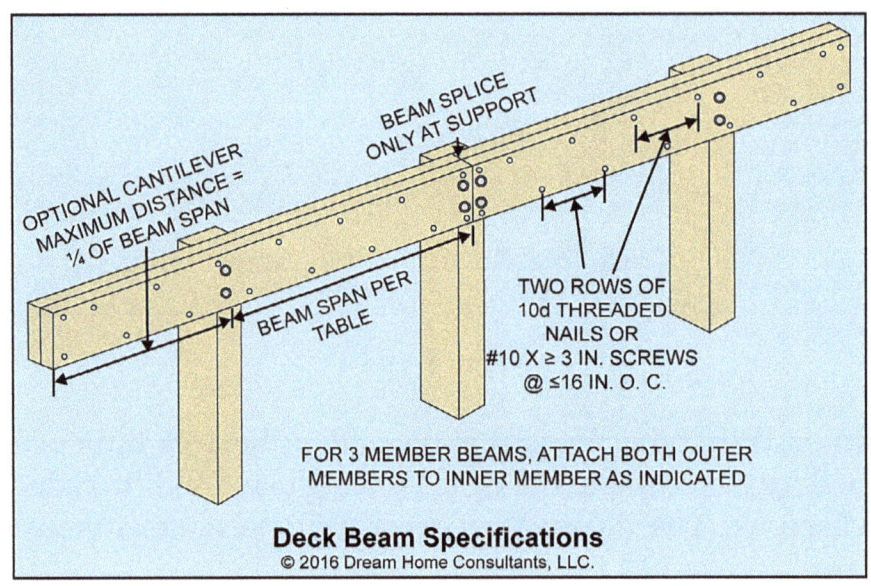

Figure 109

Deck beams should bear on top of support posts. DCA 6 and the IRC do not allow, by any method, deck beams to be fastened to the sides of support posts. Refer to Figure 110. Note that some jurisdictions allow deck beams to be bolted to the sides of support posts.

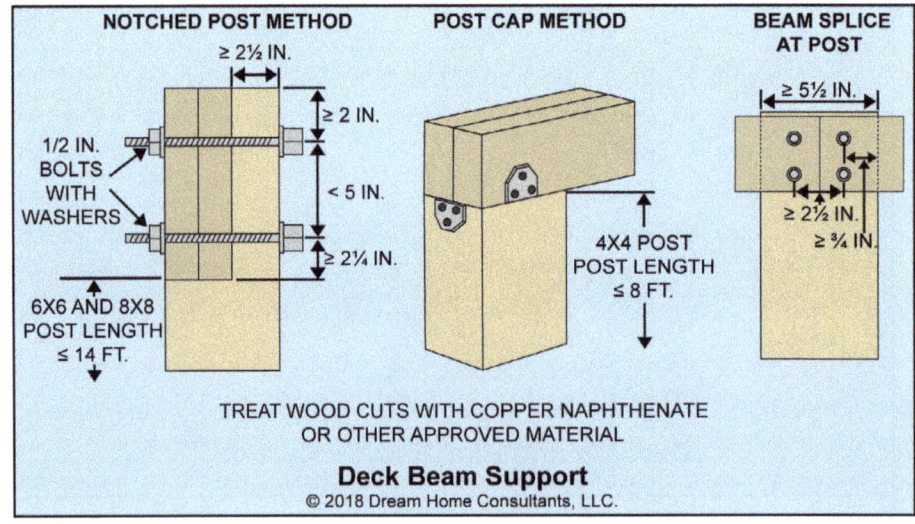

Figure 110

When deck beams, such as for framing around a cantilevered projection, are supported by a deck ledger board, the beam should be supported by a joist hanger that is attached through the deck ledger board using fasteners that penetrate fully into the building rim board or the band joist. Refer to the joist hanger manufacturer's instructions about how to install the joist hanger, including the type of fastener used to install the joist hanger. Refer to Figure 39 for an illustration.

Diagonal bracing should be installed between the corner deck support posts and the deck beam when the support post is more than 2 feet tall. DCA 6 recommends 2 x 4 braces fastened with ½-inch diameter lag screws and washers. The bracing should not be installed on posts other than the corner posts. Some jurisdictions allow other bracing methods, and they start the requirement for bracing at decks taller than 2 feet. Refer to Figure 111.

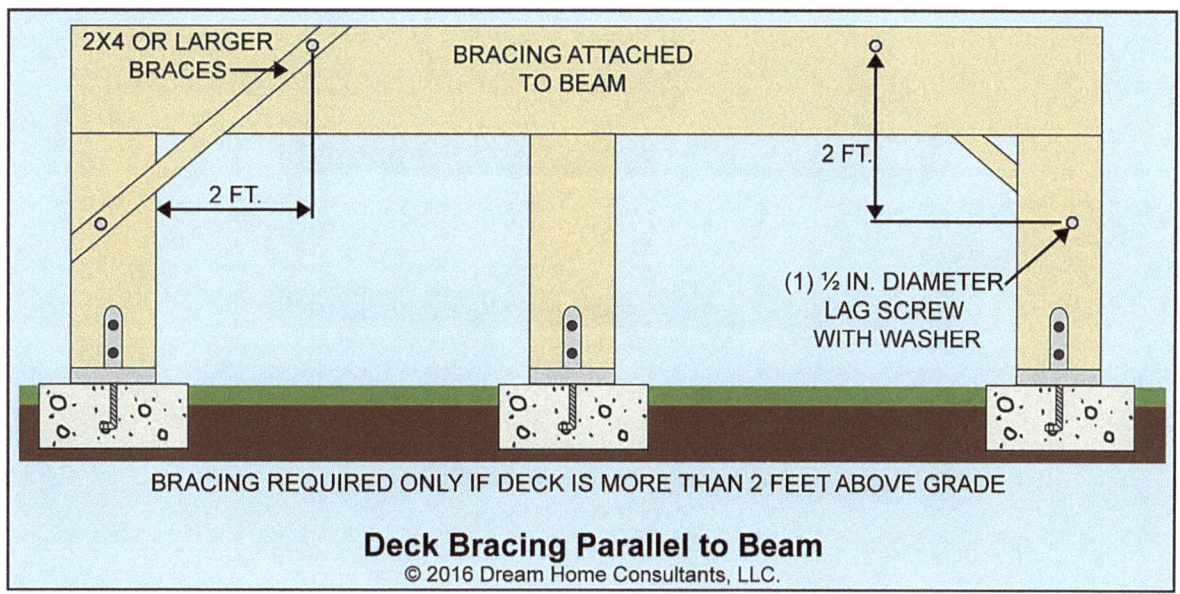

Figure 111

Deck flooring is usually installed perpendicular to the floor joists. It is occasionally installed at an angle to the floor joists for a more upscale effect. IRC 2018 provides a table (R507.7) for on-center spacing of deck joists that support deck flooring. A ⅛-inch space should be left between pieces of deck flooring to allow for expansion and for water drainage. Note that deck flooring made from materials other than dimensional lumber should be installed according to manufacturer's instructions. These materials include wood composites (such as Trex), plastic, and metal. Allowed spans for these materials, and the allowed clearances to soil, may be less than those for dimensional lumber.

Hardware, including joist hangers, angle brackets, uplift connectors, and fasteners, should be installed according to manufacturer's instructions. This includes the quantity and type of fasteners used to attach the hardware. Hardware and fasteners should be at least hot-dipped galvanized steel, and joist hangers, brackets, and connectors should be rated at least G185 or better (IRC 2018 Table R507.2.3 and R317.3.1). Hardware and fasteners located within 300 feet of salt water should be at least Grade 304 stainless steel (DCA 6-2015, IRC 2018 Table R507.2.3).

Threaded (spiral shank) nails or screws are specified for all fasteners used to build a deck, except where otherwise specified by the hardware manufacturer. Screws are not allowed as hardware fasteners, except where allowed by the manufacturer for the specific hardware model. Annular ring-shank nails may be substituted as an upgrade for threaded nails because ring-shank nails provide better withdrawal resistance.

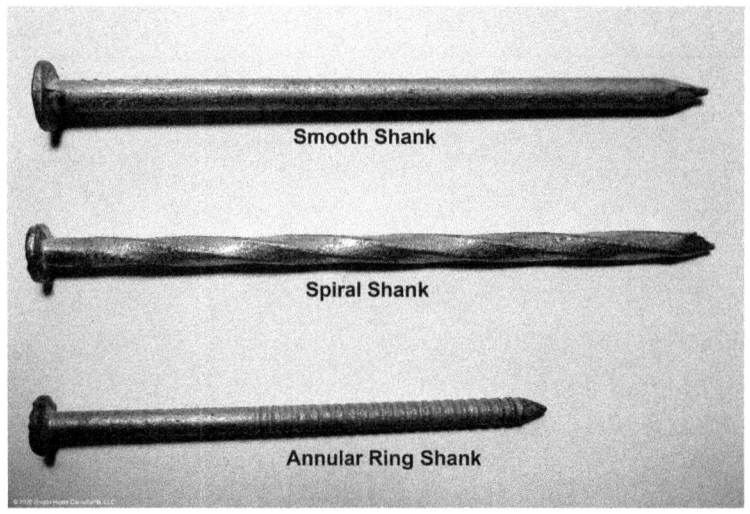

Figure 112

Use spiral shank nails, annular ring shank nails, or screws for deck fasteners, unless another fastener is specified by a deck component manufacturer's instructions.

HISTORY

The IRC did not provide specific framing details for decks until 2015, when span tables were provided for floor joists, beams, and deck flooring. Prior to IRC 2015, deck builders and government inspectors may have, **incorrectly**, used the IRC span tables that are intended for interior floor joists and beams. All editions of DCA 6 provide span tables and additional details about deck framing best practices.

The general deck framing recommendations have changed over time. Significant changes include:

- deck floor joist spans were reduced in the DCA 6-2013 update;
- deck floor joist and beam bearing on support requirements, and deck floor joist and beam connection to support requirements, were added in IRC 2018;
- a blocking requirement between cantilevered deck floor joists at the deck beam was added in IRC 2018 and DCA 6-2015;
- span tables for deck floor joists and beams, and additional deck framing details were added or revised in IRC 2018; and
- deck bracing recommendations were changed in DCA 6-2015 to remove bracing from intermediate support posts, and to use the building to provide lateral load resistance for free-standing (non-ledger) decks.

IRC 2018 deck framing requirements are located in R507.5 (beams), R507.6 (floor joists), and R507.7 (deck floor boards).

6.1 - DEFECT – DECK FLOOR JOISTS OR BEAMS OVER-SPANNED

This defect involves installing deck floor joists and deck beams with a span (distance between supports) that is more than the maximum distance in the span tables. Refer to Figures 106, 113, and 114.

This defect also includes extending deck floor joists beyond a beam (a cantilever) more than the maximum distance in the span tables. Refer to Figure 115. The span tables have changed over time, and the span tables in the IRC and in DCA 6 are different, so it is possible that deck floor joists and deck beams that do not comply with current span tables may have complied with span tables in effect when the deck was built.

Over-spanned deck floor joists and deck beams, and excessively cantilevered deck floor joists increase the risk of deck failure. The primary reason is that excessive deflection and uplift of these components can place additional loads on the hardware that holds the deck together causing the hardware to fail, thereby contributing to a deck failure. The chance of deck failure increases as the deck ages because the wood and the fasteners deteriorate due to exposure to moisture.

Over-spanned deck joists and beams usually do not create an unsafe condition by themselves. Evaluation of the situation should be recommended. Closer inspection of hardware and the deck ledger board condition is prudent.

Repair of this defect depends on the situation. Additional floor joists can usually be added to correct over-spanned floor joists. Additional posts and footings usually can be added to correct over-spanned beams.

Figure 113

Single-member beams are allowed, but their span distance is limited. The span of this single-member beam is probably too long. Note that span tables assume that the deck floor joists come from one direction, instead of coming from two directions as shown in this picture.

Figure 114

The distance between supports of this beam is probably too long. So is the distance between the guard posts. Building a deck around a tree is usually not a good idea, especially when the tree is so close to the building.

Figure 115

These deck floor joists may be cantilevered too far beyond the beam.

6.2 - DEFECT – DECK FLOOR JOISTS SUPPORTED BY FASTENERS, ANGLE BRACKET, OR LEDGER STRIP

This defect involves supporting deck floor joists only using fasteners (such as toe-nails), or using an angle bracket. Refer to Figures 117 through 119. Support of deck floor joists using only fasteners is prohibited, but is occasionally encountered, mostly on older decks.

Support using an angle bracket is common where a deck rim joist connects to the deck ledger board or to a deck beam. Support of deck floor joists (including rim joists) using angle brackets is not allowed by DCA 6 or by IRC 2018; however, it may be allowed by the angle bracket manufacturer's instructions if the angle bracket provides adequate vertical load capacity. Refer to Figure 118. Note that deck stairways impose an additional load on a deck rim joist, so support of these rim joists by nails or by angle brackets may increase the risk of stairway failure.

Support of deck floor joists by a ledger strip (usually a 2 x 2) was allowed by the IRC prior to 2018, but was not allowed by DCA 6. This support method is no longer allowed by the IRC or by DCA 6. Refer to Figure 116 to see why this method is no longer allowed by the IRC or by DCA 6.

These defects increase the risk of deck failure. The primary reason is that these support methods may not provide adequate load bearing capacity. The deck floor joists may deform or detach from the deck ledger board or from the deck beam, or they may place additional loads on the hardware that holds the deck together, thereby contributing to a deck failure. The chance of deck failure increases as the deck ages because the wood and fasteners deteriorate due to exposure to moisture.

An improperly attached floor joist usually does not create an unsafe condition by itself. Evaluation of the situation should be recommended. Closer inspection of the hardware and of the deck stairway condition is prudent.

Repair of nailed floor joists may usually be accomplished by installing joist hangers. Regular monitoring of the joists supported using angle brackets may be adequate if the angle bracket is installed according to manufacturer's instructions, including adequate vertical load capacity, and if the joist is not supporting an additional load, such as a deck stairway. Regular monitoring of joists supported by a ledger strip is usually adequate if the ledger strip is adequately fastened to the deck ledger board or to the beam, and if there is no visible evidence that the ledger strip or the deck ledger board is splitting, deteriorating, withdrawing, or deforming.

Figure 116 courtesy of Frank Woeste and Joseph Loferski

This picture demonstrates how a properly nailed 2 x 2 ledger strip fails when subjected to a load level above the 40 psf live load required by the IRC. This is new wood. Failure is more likely as the deck ages.

Figure 117

Nails, alone, are an improper method of attaching a deck floor joist to the support.

Figure 118

Some angle brackets may be rated to carry the load imposed by a deck floor joist, but angle brackets are not allowed by DCA 6 or by the IRC. If used, they should have the required fasteners installed in all round holes.

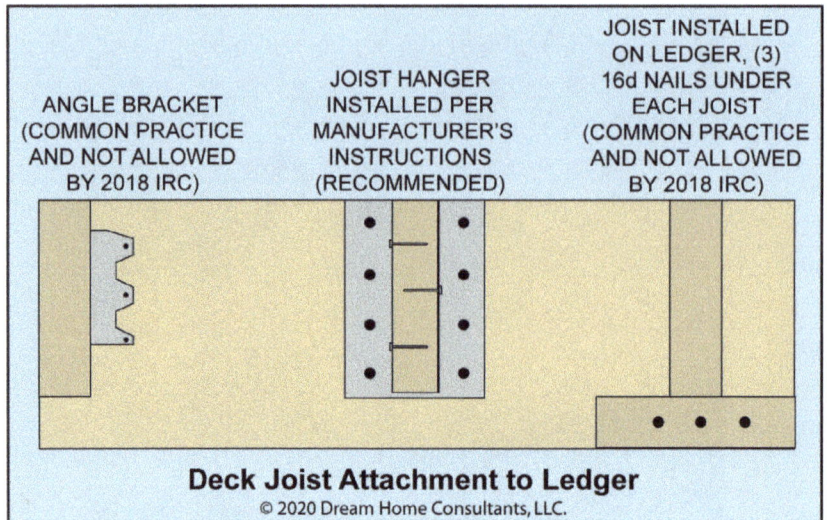

Figure 119

6.3 - DEFECT – DECK FLOOR JOISTS OR BEAMS EXCESSIVELY NOTCHED OR BORED

This defect involves cutting notches or drilling holes (boring) in deck floor joists or in beams when the holes exceed the size allowed in IRC 2018 Section 502.8. This is the same requirement as for interior floor joists. Refer to Figure 120. Measurement of notch depth is to the edge of the saw kerf (saw cut). Refer to Figure 121. The IRC 2018 and DCA 6 require field treatment of cuts with a wood preservative, such as copper naphthenate. This is rarely done.

These defects increase the risk of deck failure. The primary reason is that an excessively notched or bored joist or beam may split at the notch or at the hole, or the joist or beam may deflect under load more than it otherwise would have. Splitting and deflecting can place additional loads on the hardware that holds the deck together, thereby contributing to a deck failure. The chance of deck failure increases as the deck ages because the wood and hardware deteriorate due to exposure to moisture.

An improperly notched and bored deck floor joist or beam usually does not create an unsafe condition by itself. Evaluation of the situation should be recommended. Closer inspection of the joist, beam, and hardware condition is prudent. Regular monitoring of the joists or beams may be adequate if there is no visible evidence of wood splitting, deforming, or deteriorating.

Repair of this situation may involve installing one or more new joists next to the over-notched or over-bored member. This is often called sistering.

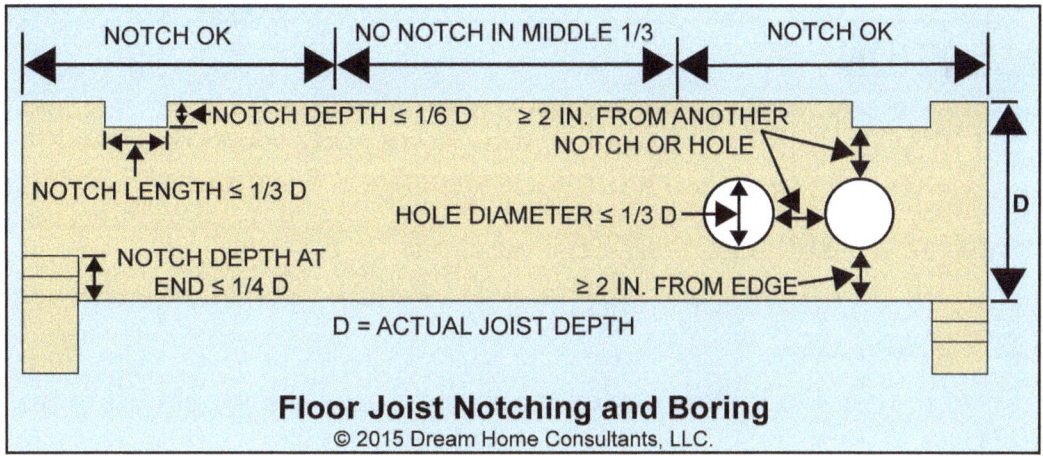

Figure 120

Figure 121

The notch is measured to the saw kerf (cut). This joist is excessively notched.

6.4 - DEFECT – IMPROPER JOIST HANGER AND CONNECTOR INSTALLATION

This defect involves failure to install joist hangers and connectors (such as uplift connectors) according to manufacturer's instructions. Common defects include:

- inadequate joist hanger vertical load capacity,
- failure to install fasteners specified by the manufacturer (Refer to Figures 122, 123, and 128.),
- failure to install a fastener in every round and oblong hole (Refer to Figure 123.),
- joist hanger or connector not approved for exterior use (Refer to Figure 125.),
- joist installed in the joist hanger seat is more than ⅛ inch from the deck ledger board or deck beam (Refer to Figure 126.),
- joist hanger flanges splayed (not flush with the joist) (Refer to Figure 122.]) and
- joist hanger or connector damaged, field-modified, or bent beyond that allowed by the manufacturer (Refer to Figures 124 and 127.).

These defects increase the risk of deck failure. The primary reason is that the joist hanger or connector may fail, or may place additional loads on the hardware that holds the deck together, thereby contributing to a deck failure. The chance of deck failure increases as the deck ages because the wood and hardware deteriorate due to exposure to moisture.

An improperly installed joist hanger or connector usually does not create an unsafe condition by itself. Evaluation of the situation should be recommended. Closer inspection of the components supported by, or connected by, the joist hanger or connector is prudent.

Repair can often be accomplished by replacing the joist hanger or connector, or by installing the correct fasteners. The joist hanger should not be reused if it is damaged during replacement. It may be necessary to install larger fasteners in any replacement joist hanger so that the new fasteners have adequate contact with the wood. This is because the original holes may be larger after the original fasteners have been removed.

6: Deck Framing 117

Figure 122

The flanges of this joist hanger should be flush against the sides of the joist. Refer to Figure 33 for a description of other defects in this picture.

Figure 123

Fasteners in the picture on the left are metal roofing screws. They are not specified by the joist hanger manufacturer to secure a joist hanger. Fasteners in the picture on the right appear to be framing gun nails and a screw. Only one type of fastener (screws or nails) should be used to secure a joist hanger, and only fasteners specified by the joist hanger manufacturer should be used.

Figure 124

This joist hanger is not supporting anything.

Figure 125

This joist hanger is not rated for exterior use. In the Simpson line, there should be a Z or an SS at the end of the joist hanger model number to indicate exterior use. The white stains indicate that the joist hanger is beginning to deteriorate.

6: Deck Framing 119

Figure 126

The member being supported (e. g., deck floor joist, truss) should not be more than ⅛ inch from the supporting member.

Figure 127

The flange of this joist hanger has been bent and is fastened to the end of the deck ledger board. The joist hanger has been damaged and is improperly installed. It may not carry the intended load.

Figure 128

Fastening a joist hanger to a block of wood such as this will not allow it to carry the intended load. The joist hanger flange on the right is not visible, so it is difficult to know how it is fastened.

6.5 - DEFECT – CANTILEVERED DECK FLOOR JOISTS NOT BLOCKED AT DECK BEAM

This defect involves failure to install full-depth blocking between cantilevered deck floor joists where the joists bear on top of the deck beam. Refer to Figure 106.

This defect increases the risk of deck failure. The primary reason is that the deck floor joists may twist at the beam, placing additional loads on the hardware that holds the deck together, thereby contributing to a deck failure. This requirement did not appear until IRC 2018 and DCA 6-2015, so blocking is unlikely to be installed on older decks.

Lack of cantilevered joist blocking does not create an unsafe condition by itself. Evaluation of the situation should be recommended. Closer inspection of the cantilevered deck floor joists and of the hardware is prudent. Regular monitoring of the deck floor joists and hardware may be adequate if there is no visible evidence of deck floor joist deformation or hardware failure.

Repair of this defect is usually accomplished by installing full-depth blocking at the beam.

6.6 - DEFECT – DECK BEAM MEMBERS NOT ADEQUATELY FASTENED TO EACH OTHER

This defect usually involves the failure to install a sufficient quantity of fasteners in multiple member beams as specified in DCA 6. This defect also involves the failure to install the recommended types of fasteners.

This defect increases the risk of deck failure. The primary reason is that the beam may not act as intended (as a single load-bearing member). Excessive deflection and deformation of the beam can place additional loads on the hardware that holds the deck together, thereby contributing to a deck failure.

An inadequately fastened beam usually does not create an unsafe condition by itself. Evaluation of the situation should be recommended. Closer inspection of the beam and the hardware condition is prudent.

Repair of this defect is usually accomplished by installing additional fasteners. Refer to Figure 109 to see the recommended pattern for installing beam fasteners.

6.7 - DEFECT – IMPROPER DECK BEAM ATTACHMENT TO THE DECK LEDGER BOARD

This defect involves supporting a beam on the deck ledger board using a nailed ledger strip, a nailed joist hanger, or an angle bracket. Refer to Figure 129.

This defect increases the risk of deck failure. The primary reason is that the deck ledger board, and these support methods, are not designed to support the additional load imposed by the beam. The deck ledger board may deform or detach from the building, or the component supporting the beam may detach from the ledger board, thereby contributing to a deck failure. The chance of failure increases as the deck ages because the wood and hardware deteriorate due to exposure to moisture.

An improperly attached beam usually does not create an unsafe condition by itself. Evaluation of the situation should be recommended. Closer inspection of the hardware, the deck beam, and the deck ledger board condition is prudent.

Repair of this defect usually may be accomplished by installing a joist hanger that is fastened through to the building band joist or rim board according to the joist hanger manufacturer's instructions. Another alternative may be independently supporting the beam.

Figure 129

The deck ledger board is not intended to support a beam. A deck ledger board should not be notched. The joist hanger supporting this beam should be one that is designed to be attached by screws or bolts that penetrate into the building band joist or rim board.

6.8 - DEFECT – DECK BEAM ATTACHED TO SIDE OF DECK POST

This defect involves supporting a deck beam on the side of the deck post, instead of on top. This defect includes using bolts, screws, nails, or joist hangers to secure the deck beam to the side of the deck post. Refer to Figures 130 and 131.

This defect increases the risk of deck failure. The primary reasons are that the fasteners could shear under load, and that the deck post or the deck beam could split where the fasteners penetrate the deck post or the deck beam. Withdrawal of fasteners is an issue when using screws as fasteners, and is a significant issue when using nails as fasteners. Nails and screws are more likely to withdraw from the post compared to bolts. The chance of failure increases as the deck ages because the wood and the hardware deteriorate due to exposure to moisture.

An improperly attached beam usually does not create an unsafe condition by itself. Evaluation of the situation should be recommended. Closer inspection of the hardware and the deck post and deck beam condition is prudent.

Repair of this defect often requires replacing the beam, and may also require replacing the posts and the footings.

Figure 130

A beam should be supported on top of the posts, not on the sides.

Figure 131

These bolts are too close to the edges of the beam. If the bolts do not shear under load, the beam might split.

6.9 - DEFECT – DECK BEAM NOT PROPERLY SECURED TO DECK POST

This defect involves failure to secure the deck beam on the top of the deck post by using machine bolts or a post cap.

This defect increases the risk of deck failure. The primary reason is that the beam could be moved off of the post either by lateral movement or by uplift of the deck. Note that some jurisdictions permit the use of nails to secure the beam to deck posts below a certain height (such as 4 feet).

An improperly attached beam usually does not create an unsafe condition by itself. Evaluation of the situation should be recommended. Closer inspection of the hardware and of the deck post and deck beam is prudent.

Repair of this defect may involve installing a retrofit post cap to secure the deck beam to the deck post.

6.10 - DEFECT – DECK BEAM NOT SUPPORTED BY DECK POST

This defect involves failure to support the deck beam on a deck post, or on a component that is designed to bear the load imposed by the deck beam. Examples include using rafters, stringers, and braces to support a deck beam.

This defect increases the risk of deck failure. Refer to Figures 132 through 134. The primary reason is that the support component could deflect, deform, or fail under load. Excessive deflection and deformation of the support component can place additional loads on hardware used to hold the deck together, causing the hardware to fail, thereby contributing to a deck failure. The chance of failure increases as the deck ages because the wood and hardware deteriorate due to exposure to moisture.

An improperly supported beam usually may not create an unsafe condition by itself. Evaluation of the situation should be recommended. Closer inspection of the entire deck is prudent.

Repair of this defect depends on the situation.

Figure 132

A deck that is supported by a roof should be designed by an engineer.

6: Deck Framing

Figure 133

As shown on the left, a deck supported by a stairway stringer is very likely to fail. As shown on the right, this deck is failing.

Figure 134

A deck supported only by struts such as these is likely to fail.

6.11 - DEFECT – SPLICE IN MULTIPLE-MEMBER DECK BEAM IS NOT SUPPORTED BY A DECK POST

This defect involves failure to install a post at the joint where different members of a multiple-member beam meet. Refer to Figure 135.

This defect increases the risk of deck failure. The primary reason is that the beam may deflect or deform at the joint. They may place additional loads on hardware used to hold the beam and the deck together causing the hardware to fail, thereby contributing to a deck failure.

An improperly supported beam splice may not often create an unsafe condition by itself. Evaluation of the situation should be recommended. Closer inspection of the beam, deck post, and hardware is prudent.

Repair of this defect may involve installing a post and a footing under the splice in the beam.

Figure 135

A post and a footing should be installed under this splice in the beam.

6.12 - DEFECT – DECK BRACING DEFECTS

Deck bracing defects are difficult to evaluate because of the wide variety of approved bracing materials and methods over time, and among jurisdictions. About the only bracing methods that are likely to be consistently incorrect are the lack of bracing on decks with posts taller than between about 2 feet and 4 feet tall, bracing that is not attached to the beam, and bracing secured only by nails. Refer to Figures 111 and 136.

Bracing defects increase the risk of deck failure. The primary reason is that the deck may move under loads, such as wind or people moving on the deck. This may place additional loads on the deck hardware used to hold the deck together causing the hardware to fail, and contributing to a deck failure. The chance of failure increases as the deck ages because the wood and hardware deteriorate due to exposure to moisture.

An inadequately braced deck usually does not create an unsafe condition by itself. Evaluation of the situation should be recommended. Closer inspection of the hardware, deck post, and deck beam is prudent.

Repair of absent and unapproved deck bracing is to install approved bracing. Repair for bracing that was approved by earlier versions of DCA 6, or that is approved by the local jurisdiction is not required.

Figure 136

These braces are not secured to the deck, and should not be secured to intermediate posts.

6.13 - DEFECT – DECK FLOORING DEFECTS

This defect involves failure to install deck flooring according to IRC or DCA 6 requirements, or according to manufacturer's instructions. Common defects include:

- flooring over-spanned,
- failure to install approved fastener type or quantity,
- failure to leave an approximately ⅛-inch space between flooring boards, and
- installing fasteners below the surface of the flooring material (creating a water trap that can cause premature deterioration of the material) (Refer to Figure 137.).

Flooring defects can increase the risk of deck failure, but this is uncommon. These defects usually result only in cosmetic issues. These defects can, however, cause conditions such as trip and fall hazards and splinter hazards if the flooring lifts up from the deck floor joists. These defects can cause injury if the flooring fails under load.

Flooring defects usually do not create an unsafe condition; however, trip and fall hazards created by uneven flooring may be considered an unsafe condition. Regular monitoring of the flooring is usually adequate. Repair, if necessary, depends on the situation.

Figure 137

Lack of a space between floor boards, and over-driven fasteners may cause these floor boards to deteriorate prematurely.

6.14 - DEFECT – DETERIORATED AND DAMAGED DECK FRAMING AND HARDWARE

This defect category includes several common defects. Refer to the discussions about wood and hardware deterioration in the Deck Ledger Attachment to the Building chapter for additional discussion about deteriorated wood and hardware. These defects include:

- visibly deteriorated (rotted), and visibly damaged wood (Refer to Figure 138.); and
- hardware presenting significant red rust.

Deteriorated and damaged wood and hardware increase the risk of deck failure. The primary reason is that the wood and the hardware may be weakened to the point where connections can place additional loads on hardware used to hold the deck together causing the hardware to fail, thereby contributing to a deck failure. The chance of failure increases as the deck ages because the wood and hardware deteriorate due to exposure to moisture.

Deteriorated and damaged deck floor joists, beams, or hardware create an unsafe condition. Action to correct these defects should be recommended.

Repair methods depend on the situation. Replacing deteriorated or damaged members and hardware may be an option if the condition is not widespread, and if the deck is within its expected service life. Replacement of the entire deck may be a more cost-effective option if the condition is widespread, or if the deck is at or beyond the end of its expected service life.

6: Deck Framing

Figure 138 courtesy of Randy Sipe

This deck flooring is severely deteriorated.

Photo courtesy of Jerrod Turnbow

What could possibly go wrong? Read Chapter 7 to find out.

7: DECK POSTS AND FOOTINGS

OVERVIEW

Deck posts and footings should provide structurally-stable and long-lasting support for the deck.

IMPLICATIONS OF DECK POST AND FOOTING FAILURE

Deck failures caused only by deck post and footing defects are uncommon. It is more likely that a deck post and footing defect combines with another deck component defect, such as a deck ledger attachment defect, or a deck framing defect, to contribute to failure of the deck. Deck post and footing defects, by themselves, are unlikely to cause an unsafe condition. Deck post and footing defects should, however, be reported when encountered. Action should be taken to address these defects.

GENERAL DECK POST AND FOOTING REQUIREMENTS

IRC 2018, in Section 507.4, permits wood deck post height up to 8 feet tall for most 4 x 4 deck posts, and up to 14 feet tall for 6 x 6 and 8 x 8 deck posts. DCA 6 restricts wood deck posts to 6 x 6 or larger up to 14 feet tall. Deck beams are required to bear on top of the deck posts, so 4 x 4 posts may not provide enough surface area to support other than 2-ply deck beams. Note that maximum deck post height may be less for larger decks, and for wood species other than Southern Pine.

Steel deck posts (columns) have been allowed by IRC Section R407.3 since the 2000 edition. Steel posts must be at least Schedule 40 thickness and at least 3 inches in diameter. Maximum steel deck post height requires engineering analysis.

Deck posts should be located near the center of the footing. Deck posts should be restrained from movement at the bottom of the post, and at the top of the post.

Footings for a deck should extend below the local frost line if the deck is supported by a deck ledger board that is attached to the building. This requirement does not apply to free-standing (non-ledger) decks; however, placing deck footings below the frost line is best practice for all decks.

Deck footing area and thickness are based on the number of square feet of deck supported by the footing (tributary area), soil load-bearing value, and the local ground snow load. The IRC 2018 footing table (R507.3.1), and the DCA 6-2015 footing table (Table 4) provide different footing sizes. Refer to Figure 139, which illustrates how to calculate tributary area in order to determine footing size.

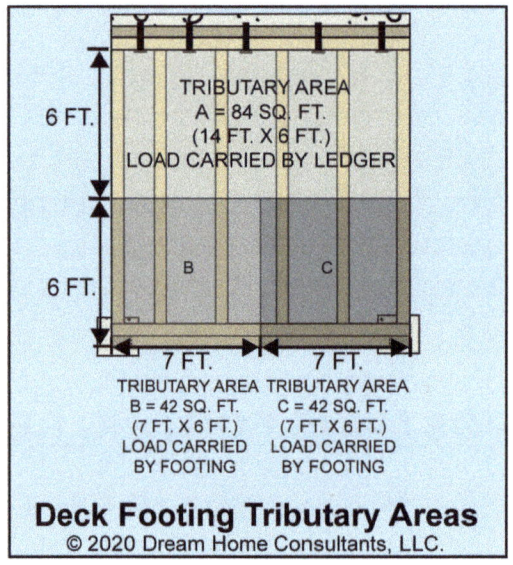

Figure 139

IRC 2018 and DCA 6-2015 provide similar, but not identical, options for connecting the deck post to the deck beam, and for restraining the deck post at the footing. The recommended methods for restraining the deck post at the footing involve extending the footing above the soil and connecting the footing to the post using a manufactured post base. Allowed methods involve embedding the post in the soil, and embedding the post in a concrete footing. While these methods are allowed, they are not recommended because it is likely that the post and the post base will eventually deteriorate, especially in damp environments. Refer to Figures 140, 141, and 151.

7: Deck Posts and Footings   135

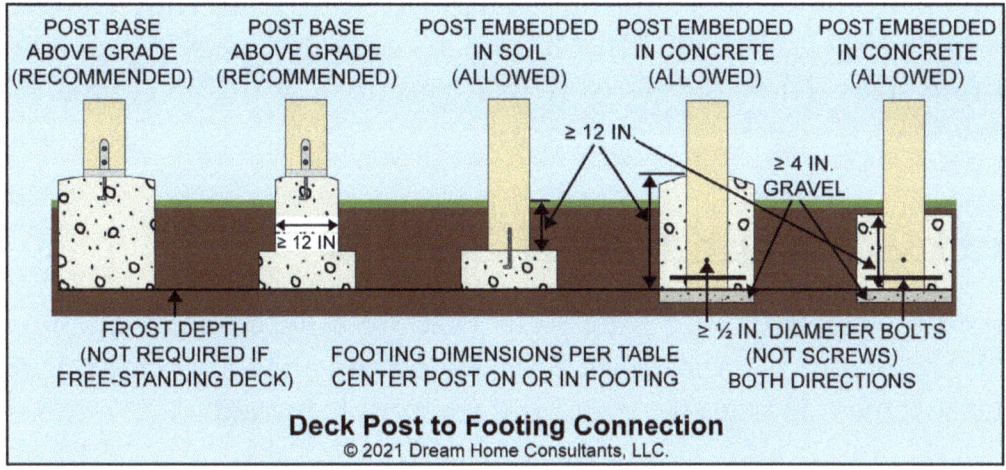

Figure 140

Figure 141

This post base is only a few weeks old, and will eventually be buried. It is already showing white rust, which is an indication that the galvanization is beginning to deteriorate.

HISTORY

The IRC did not provide specific deck post details until IRC 2015, in which post size and length, and post connection to the beam and to the footing, were addressed. Prior to 2015 the IRC addressed post size in the foundation section (R407.3). IRC 2018 addresses deck posts in R507.4.

All editions of DCA 6 provide specific details about post size, post length, and post connection to the beam and footing. These details were changed in DCA 6-2015 as compared to earlier editions.

The IRC did not provide deck footing sizes until IRC 2018, in which a footing size table was included (Table R507.3.1). All editions of DCA 6 provide specific details about footing sizes. These details were changed in DCA 6-2015 compared to earlier editions.

7.1 - DEFECT – DECK POST TOO TALL

This defect involves installing deck posts that are taller than the recommended height. Measurement is from the top of the footing to the bottom of the deck beam. Measurement is from the ground if the post is buried.

Deck posts that are too tall increase the risk of deck failure. The primary reason is that excessive post deflection and deformation can place additional loads on hardware used to hold the deck together causing the hardware to fail, thereby contributing to a deck failure

Deck posts that are too tall usually do not create an unsafe condition by themselves. Evaluation of the situation should be recommended. Closer inspection of the post, the deck hardware, the deck ledger, and the deck beam condition is prudent.

Repair of this defect usually requires installing larger posts, and often requires installing larger footings. Replacement of deck posts that were approved by earlier versions of DCA 6, or that were approved by the local jurisdiction is usually not required without visual evidence of post deformation or potential hardware failure.

7.2 - DEFECT – DECK POST NATURAL DEFECTS

Defects such as shakes, checks, splits, and bows are common, and are allowed, with limits, for wood deck posts. The following are limits for #2 grade, 4 x 4, Southern Pine posts. Limits are different for other species and larger posts.

- **Shake** (separation along the grain)

    Surface shakes do not run through to another surface.
    Limit: ≤ 3feet long, or ≤ ¼ of the post length (Refer to Figure 142.).

    Through shakes run through to another surface.
    Limit: ≤ 2 feet long. It is a split if at the end of the post.

- **Check** (separation across the grain)

    Surface checks do not run through to another surface. No limits.

    Through checks run through to another surface. No limits unless at end of post, then it is a split.

- **Split** (separation along the grain that runs through to another surface)
    Limit: length ≤ 1.5 times post width.

- **Bow** (post curves from top to bottom in one plane)
    Limit: bow measured from a straight line runs from ¾ inch for an 8-foot tall post to 3 ¼ inches for a 14-foot tall post

Deck posts that have natural defects greater than the maximum allowed amount increase the risk of deck failure. The primary reason is that excessive post deflection and deformation can place additional loads on hardware used to hold the deck together causing the hardware to fail, thereby contributing to a deck failure.

Deck posts that have excessive natural defects usually do not create an unsafe condition by themselves. Evaluation of the situation should be recommended. Closer inspection of the hardware and the deck beam condition is prudent. Repair of this defect usually requires replacing the defective posts.

Figure 142

This shake is too long. The post is no longer #2 grade.

7.3 - DEFECT – DECK POST NOT PLUMB

Deck posts should be plumb, however, many are not perfectly plumb. There is no generally accepted standard stating how far out-of-plumb is unacceptable. One guideline is ⅛-inch in 8 feet. Refer to Figure 143.

Deck posts that are significantly out-of-plumb increase the risk of deck failure. The primary reason is that the post could fail under load. It is possible that the post was installed out-of-plumb. It is possible that the post has moved out of plumb due to deck movement. A post that has moved is, potentially, a serious situation.

Deck posts that are not plumb usually do not create an unsafe condition by themselves. Evaluation of the situation should be recommended. Closer inspection of the post, the post base, the post cap, and the deck beam condition is prudent, especially for posts that are out of plumb beyond the guideline. Inspection for deck lateral movement is also prudent for significantly out-of-plumb posts.

Repair of posts installed out-of-plumb usually requires repositioning the post, and may require replacing the footing. Repair of posts that have moved out-of-plumb requires determining the cause of the movement, repairing the cause, then dealing with the post and the footing.

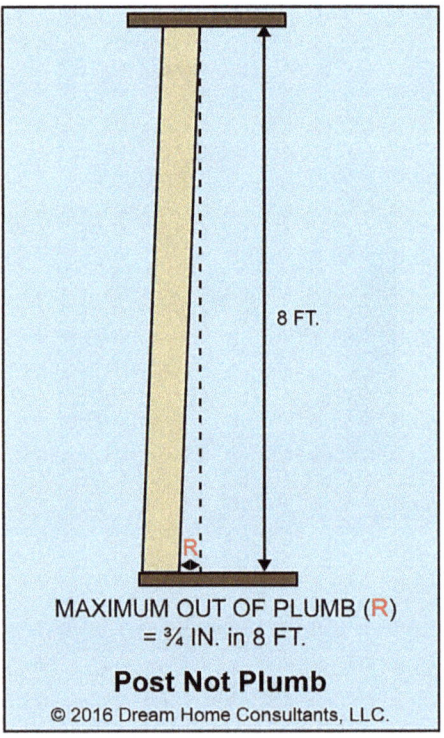

Figure 143

7.4 - DEFECT – DECK POST NOT IN CENTER OF FOOTING

Deck posts should be located in the center one-third of the footing. There is no generally accepted standard stating how far out of the center one-third of the footing is unacceptable. Refer to Figure 144.

Deck posts that are not in the center one-third of the footing increase the risk of deck failure. The primary reason is that the footing could move or crack, causing the post to move, thereby contributing to a deck failure.

Deck posts that are not in the center one-third of the footing do not create an unsafe condition by themselves. Evaluation of the situation should be recommended.

Repair may involve replacing the footing.

Figure 144

This post is not in the center of the footing. The footing is probably too small, too thin, and too close to the foundation wall. In addition, the post base is significantly deteriorated.

7.5 - DEFECT – DECK POST NOT SECURED AT THE BOTTOM OF THE POST

Deck posts should be secured at the bottom of the post using an approved method. The preferred method is to use a post base that is secured to a footing, the top of which is above the ground. Posts are allowed to be secured by embedding the post in the ground, or by embedding the post in concrete. Refer to Figure 140. Embedding posts in the ground and embedding them in concrete are not recommended because the posts will deteriorate due to constant exposure to moisture.

Deck posts that are not secured at the bottom of the post increase the risk of deck failure. The primary reason is that the post could move off of the footing and contribute to a deck failure.

Deck posts that are not secured at the bottom of the post do not create an unsafe condition by themselves. Evaluation of the situation should be recommended. Closer inspection of the hardware and the deck post condition is prudent.

Repair of posts that are not secured at the bottom of the post usually involves installing a retrofit post base, assuming that the footing is adequate in area and in thickness.

Figure 145

This angle bracket is not an approved post base, and does not adequately restrain the post against movement.

7.6 - DEFECT – DECK FOOTING TOO SMALL OR DAMAGED

Deck footings transfer loads from the deck to the soil. Deck footings that are too small in area, that are too thin, or that are damaged increase the risk of deck failure. Refer to Figures 146 through 149. The primary reason is that the footing could crack or settle under load and cause the post to move, thereby contributing to a deck failure.

Deck footings that are too small, too thin, or that are damaged usually do not create an unsafe condition by themselves. Evaluation of the situation should be recommended. Closer inspection of the hardware and ot the deck post is prudent.

Repair of this defect involves replacing the footing, and may require replacing the post.

Figure 146

Most patio slabs are too thin to serve as a deck footing.

Figure 147

This footing is probably too small, and may be too thin.

Figure 148

The fact that this deck post is not in the center one-third of the footing may be part of the cause of this footing damage.

7: Deck Posts and Footings   143

Figure 149

Retaining walls should not be used as deck footings.

7.7 - DEFECT – DECK FOOTING WITHIN FIVE FEET FROM THE BUILDING FOUNDATION

A deck footing that is within five feet from the building foundation should be installed so that the bottom of the deck footing is at or below the bottom of the building footing. Doing so avoids imposing the load carried by the deck footing onto the building footing.

Deck footings that are within five feet from the building foundation increase the risk of damage to the building foundation. The primary reason is that the load imposed on the building foundation by the deck footing could damage the building foundation. Refer to Figure 150.

Deck footings that are within five feet from the building foundation do not create an unsafe condition. Evaluation of the situation should be recommended. Evaluation will require determining whether the bottom of the deck footing is at or below the level of the building foundation footing.

Repair of this defect usually involves replacing the footing, and may require replacing the post.

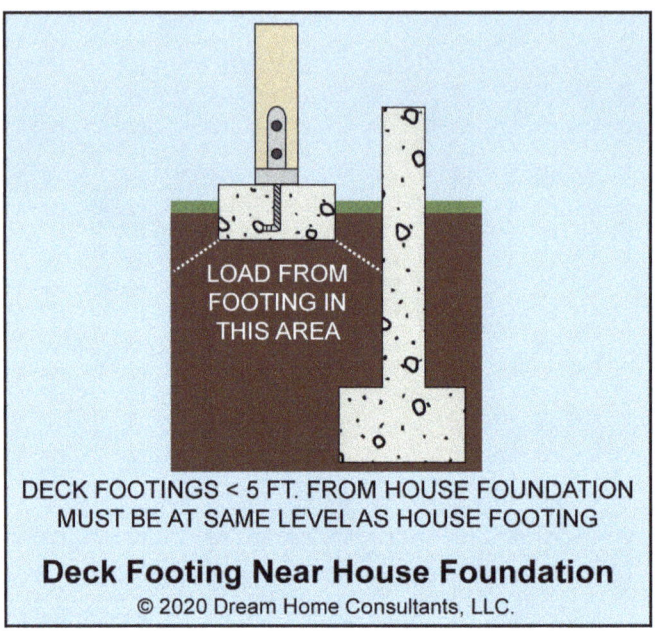

Figure 150

7.8 - DEFECT – DETERIORATED AND DAMAGED DECK POSTS AND HARDWARE

This defect category includes several common defects. Refer to the discussions about wood and hardware deterioration in the Deck Ledger Attachment to the Building chapter for additional discussion about deteriorated wood and hardware. These defects include:

- visibly deteriorated (rotted), and visibly damaged wood (Refer to Figure 151.); and
- hardware presenting significant red rust.

Deteriorated and damaged wood and deteriorated and damaged hardware increase the risk of deck failure. The primary reasons include that deteriorated and damaged wood and deteriorated and damaged hardware can fail. They can also place additional loads on the hardware used to hold the deck together causing the hardware to fail, thereby contributing to a deck failure

Deteriorated and damaged deck posts and deteriorated and damaged hardware create an unsafe condition. Action to correct these defects should be recommended. Repair usually involves replacing the post, and may involve replacing the footing.

7: Deck Posts and Footings   145

Figure 151-1

Figure 151-2

Posts buried in the ground will eventually deteriorate in damp environments.

8: DECK ELECTRICAL REQUIREMENTS

OVERVIEW

The IRC requires installing a light at a deck served by a stairway, or at a deck that has a door to the deck that provides access to grade. The IRC also requires installing a receptacle at a deck if a door opens to the deck. These requirements are intended to improve safety and convenience for people using the deck.

The IRC requires that decks have adequate clearance between the deck and overhead sources of electricity, such as electrical service wires and broadband cable wires. Clearance is not required to overhead telephone wires.

IMPLICATIONS OF DECK ELECTRICAL REQUIREMENTS FAILURE

The primary implication of failing to install a light at a deck is a trip and fall hazard if the deck or deck stairway is used in low light conditions. The primary implications of failing to install a receptacle at a deck is electrical shock; it is also a fire hazard. Use of extension cords to provide electricity to a deck can be a shock and a fire hazard if the cord becomes damaged, and if the cord is supplied by a receptacle that is not protected by a ground fault circuit interrupter (GFCI).

GENERAL DECK ELECTRICAL REQUIREMENTS

DCA 6 cites the IRC stairway light requirements. The IRC requires a light at the top landing of exterior stairways, and at exterior doors with access to grade. This requirement is usually interpreted to require installing a light at the door that opens to the deck, regardless of whether the deck is served by a stairway. The light serving the deck is often next to the door to the deck, but the light may be located anywhere within the perimeter of the deck. The light should provide reasonable illumination of the entire stairway.

8: Deck Electrical Requirements

The IRC requires a 120-volt GFCI-protected 15-amp, or 20-amp receptacle somewhere within the perimeter of the deck if a door opens to the deck. This receptacle should be protected with a damp area cover (older decks) or a wet area (bubble-type) cover (newer decks).

HISTORY

The exterior stairway and exterior door light requirements have been in the IRC since the 2000 edition, and were also in most legacy codes. The requirements have not changed substantially.

The requirement to install a 120-volt receptacle at a deck first appeared in IRC 2009. The required receptacle on the rear wall of the building was often installed at the deck, but until IRC 2009 there was no specific requirement to do so.

8.1 - DEFECT – ABSENT DECK-RELATED LIGHTING

Absent deck-related lighting creates an unsafe condition, especially if the deck is served by a stairway. Action to correct the situation should be recommended. Repair of this defect involves installing a switch-controlled light to illuminate the deck and the stairway. Note that there is no requirement about how much light should be provided to the deck or to the stairway.

8.2 - DEFECT – ABSENT DECK-RELATED RECEPTACLE

An absent deck-related receptacle may create an unsafe condition. Evaluation of the situation should be recommended. For decks built before about 2009, a potentially acceptable, but not ideal, solution is to serve the deck from a nearby GFCI protected receptacle. Repair of this defect for decks built after about 2009 involves installing a GFCI-protected receptacle within the perimeter of the deck. Note that this receptacle may not be supplied from the 120 volt, 20-amp, kitchen receptacle circuits.

8.3 - DEFECT – INADEQUATE CLEARANCE TO OVERHEAD ELECTRICAL WIRES

This defect involves wires carrying electricity that someone may be able to reach while using the deck. These wires include 120/240 volt overhead electrical service wires and network-powered broadband cable wires. These overhead electric service and network-powered broadband cable wires should be at least ten feet above the deck, or at least three feet horizontally from the deck. These wires do not include telephone service wires and fiber optic cables. Refer to Figure 152.

Electrical wires that can be reached from the deck create an unsafe condition. Evaluation of the situation should be recommended.

Repair of this defect usually involves moving the wires.

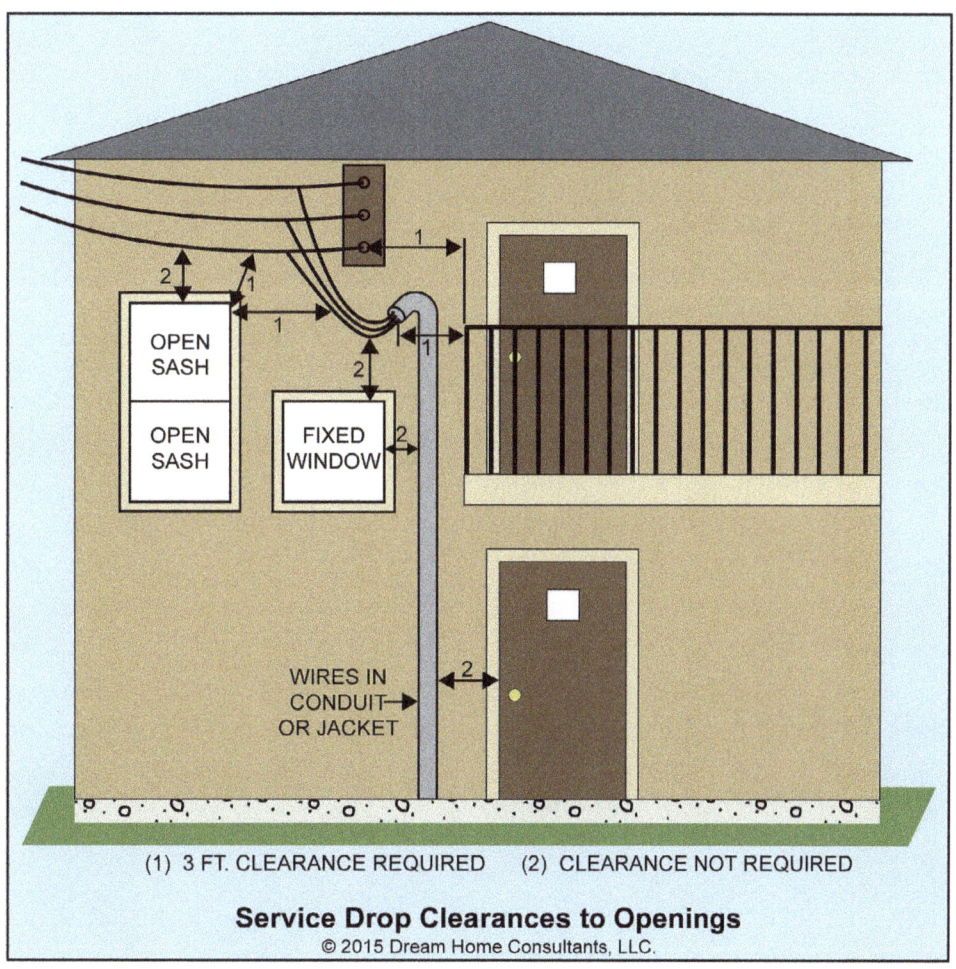

Figure 152

APPENDIX A: DECK EVALUATION PROTOCOL

The following is a suggested protocol for evaluating a deck for compensation using the ASHI Deck Standard of Practice and the Deck Evaluation Checklist in this book. People should develop their own protocol based on factors such as local regulations and customs, assessment of deck evaluation risks, and expertise/comfort level in evaluating decks.

1. Identify decks to be evaluated, including factors such as estimated deck age, deck area, deck height above grade, accessibility of deck components including both the top of the deck and under the deck, accessibility of building components to which the deck is attached, and the presence of a stairway.

2. Identify the deck construction guidelines to be used when evaluating the decks. Typical deck construction guidelines include DCA 6, the IRC, and local deck building codes.

3. Obtain a written deck evaluation agreement signed by the client.

4. Determine if the deck and the deck stairs, if any, appear safe to use during the evaluation.

5. Verify accessibility of deck and building components, and report and disclaim evaluation of inaccessible components.

6. Evaluate the decks by comparing the decks the identified deck construction guidelines.

7. Prepare and present the written deck evaluation report.

The following are definitions that people may wish to use when evaluating decks.

- **Acceptable (Accept., A)** means that the component complies with the deck construction guidelines, and that the component appears to be functioning properly at the time of the evaluation. Acceptable defects, if any, appear cosmetic and do not appear to negatively affect the performance of the component.

- **Unacceptable (Unaccept., U)** means that the component does not comply with the deck construction guidelines, or that the component does not appear to be functioning properly at the time of the evaluation.

- **Unsafe (Unsafe, UN)** means that the inspector believes that the component is unsafe according to the definition of unsafe in this book.

- **End of Service Life (End Life, EL)** means the inspector believes that the component is near or at the end of its expected service life. Estimating service life is a judgment call, and is based on factors such as the visible condition of the component and the environment in which the component is installed. Service life can vary from a few years in a marine (saltwater) environment to 20 to 30 years in a dry environment.

- **Not Inspected (Not Insp., NI)** means that the component was present but was not inspected. Report the reasons why the component was not inspected, recommend that someone inspect the component, and advise that defects may exist.

- **Evaluate (Eval., E)** means that the component should be evaluated by a qualified specialist to determine the condition of the component and what, if any, action should be taken to address any component deficiency. Additional evaluation should be recommended when evaluation of a component by the inspector is beyond the scope of the deck evaluation, or when evaluation requires expertise, tools, or equipment that are beyond the scope of the deck evaluation. Examples of qualified specialists include engineers and contractors.

- **Act (Act, AC)** means that the inspector believes that the deck owner should act to address the defect. Repair or replacement of the components are two common actions. A qualified engineer, contractor, or other specialist may recommend another action.

APPENDIX B: ASHI DECK INSPECTION STANDARD OF PRACTICE

AMERICAN SOCIETY OF HOME INSPECTORS AUXILIARY STANDARD OF PROFESSIONAL PRACTICE FOR RESIDENTIAL DECK INSPECTIONS

1. PURPOSE OF THIS STANDARD

1.1 The purpose of this Auxiliary Standard of Professional Practice for Residential Deck Inspections (Deck Standard) is to establish a voluntary standard for inspectors who perform a fee-for-service residential deck inspection. This Deck Standard does not apply to inspection of a residential deck performed during a home inspection using The ASHI Standard of Practice for Home Inspections (ASHI SoP). A residential deck inspection performed using this Deck Standard is an additional service that is a more thorough and detailed inspection of residential deck components than is performed using the ASHI SoP.

1.2 This Deck Standard does not limit inspectors from:

  A. including other services or components in addition to those required by this Deck Standard; and

  B. excluding residential deck components from a residential deck inspection, if agreed to in writing by the client.

1.3 An inspector who performs a residential deck inspection using this Deck Standard shall adhere to the ASHI® Code of Ethics for the Home Inspection Profession.

2. RESIDENTIAL DECK INSPECTION OBJECTIVE AND SCOPE

2.1 The objectives of a residential deck inspection are to:

  A. determine if, at the time of the residential deck inspection, the inspected residential deck components substantially conform to a deck construction guideline selected by the inspector; the inspector may select more than one deck construction guideline; and

  B. identify residential deck components that are unsafe, or are near the end of their expected service lives at the time of the residential deck inspection.

2.2 A residential deck inspection performed using this Deck Standard:

   A. is not technically exhaustive;

   B. is general and does not include:

   1. government laws and regulations, except those contained in a deck construction guideline selected by the inspector,

   2. manufacturer's installation instructions; and

   C. does not provide a warranty or guarantee regarding the condition of the inspected residential deck.

3. INSPECTION AND REPORT

3.1 The inspector, using the inspector's professional judgment, shall determine and identify:

   A. one or more deck construction guidelines that the inspector will use during the residential deck inspection; and

   B. the residential decks that shall be inspected during the residential deck inspection.

3.2 The inspector shall inspect the readily accessible, visually observable, installed residential deck components specified in this Deck Standard.

3.3 The inspector shall issue a written report, using a medium and a format selected by the inspector, that:

   A. identifies the determinations made in 3.1;

   B. identifies residential deck components that, in the professional judgment of the inspector, do not substantially conform to the deck construction guidelines selected by the inspector, are unsafe, or that are near the end of their expected service lives;

   C. provides the reasoning or explanation as to the nature of the deficiencies reported in 3.3.B that are not self-evident;

   D. recommends correction, further evaluation, or monitoring of residential deck components identified in 3.3.B; and

   E. identifies residential deck components specified for inspection in this Deck Standard that were present during the inspection but were not inspected and a reason why they were not inspected.

4. FLASHING

4.1 The inspector shall inspect the visible:

1. residential deck ledger flashing for decks attached to the building,

2. flashing at doors that open on to the residential deck, and

3. flashing and sealants where residential deck components penetrate the wall covering.

5. DECK LEDGER

5.1 This section applies only when the residential deck is attached to the building.

5.2 The inspectors shall inspect the visible:

1. deck ledger board,

2. fasteners that attach the deck ledger board to the building,

3. lateral load connectors,

4. building rim joist or rim board at the location where the deck ledger board is attached to the building,

5. building floor joists or floor trusses at the location where the deck ledger board is attached to the building, and

6. building foundation, at the location where the deck ledger board is attached to the foundation.

6. FLOOR SYSTEM

6.1 The inspector shall inspect the visible:

1. floor joists, including connections to beams and deck ledgers,

2. rim joists,

3. beams,

4. fasteners, connectors, and similar residential deck components, and

5. decking/planking and similar residential deck components.

7. POSTS, COLUMNS, AND FOOTINGS

7.1 The inspector shall inspect the visible:

1. posts, columns, and similar residential deck components,

2. fasteners, connectors, and similar residential deck components, and

3. footings.

8. BRACING

8.1 The inspector shall inspect the visible:

1. bracing members, and

2. fasteners, connectors, and similar residential deck components.

9. GUARDS AND HANDRAILS

9.1 The inspector shall inspect the visible:

1. guards and stair guards,

2. handrails,

3. guard and handrail support posts,

4. guard and handrail in-fill residential deck components, and

5. fasteners, connectors, and similar residential deck components.

10. STAIRS

10.1 The inspector shall inspect the visible stair and step:

1. stringers, including their connection to the residential deck,

2. stringer support posts,

3. risers,

4. treads,

5. landings, and

6. fasteners, connectors, and similar residential deck components.

11. OTHER COMPONENTS

11.1 The inspector shall report the presence of suspected excessive loads such as spas and hot tubs.

11.2 The inspector shall report the absence of exterior light fixtures where recommended.

12. GENERAL LIMITATIONS AND EXCLUSIONS

A. The inspector is NOT required to perform actions, make determinations, identify or report about residential deck components, or make recommendations unless specifically required by this Deck Standard.

B. Residential deck inspections performed using this Deck Standard are NOT required to identify or to report:

1. conditions including, but not limited to, vertical and lateral loads imposed by people, property, and acts of god such as earthquakes, flooding, snow, and wind,

2. latent defects, consequential damages, and cosmetic issues,

3. residential deck components that are concealed or otherwise not visible, or that are NOT readily accessible,

4. the condition of components that are not residential deck components, and

5. residential deck components that were NOT inspected by reason of 12.D.6.

C. The inspector is NOT required to determine:

1. strength, adequacy, effectiveness, structural integrity, and efficiency of any residential deck component, including structural components,

2. manufacturer, species, grade, type, and effectiveness of preservative treatment, and similar characteristics of lumber and other residential deck components, unless this information is clearly visible, readable, and readily accessible during the residential deck inspection,

3. type, application method, and level of corrosion resistance applied to fasteners, connectors, and similar residential deck components, unless this information is clearly visible, readable, and readily accessible, during the residential deck inspection,

4. type, length, and other characteristics of fasteners unless this information is clearly visible, readable, and readily accessible during the residential deck inspection,

5. if cuts in preservative treated lumber have been field-treated with a preservative,

6. methods, materials, and costs of corrections,

7. future conditions including, but not limited to, residential deck component failure and the remaining life expectancy of residential deck components,

8. presence of plants, animals, and other life forms and substances that may be hazardous or harmful to humans including, but not limited to, wood destroying organisms, molds and mold-like substances,

9. presence of environmental hazards including, but not limited to, allergens, toxins, carcinogens, electromagnetic radiation, noise, radioactive substances, and contaminants in building materials, soil, water, and air,

10. soil conditions relating to geotechnical or hydrologic specialties,

11. whether any item, material, condition, or residential deck component is subject to recall, controversy, litigation, product liability or other adverse claim or condition, and

12. compliance of residential deck components with past requirements and guidelines (codes, regulations, laws, ordinances, specifications, installation and maintenance instructions, use and care guides, etc.).

D. The inspector is NOT required to:

1. perform any act or service contrary to law or regulation;

2. perform architectural, engineering, or surveying services, or to confirm or evaluate such services performed by others;

3. perform any trade or any professional service other than as required in this Deck Standard;

4. provide warranties or guarantees of any kind;

5. inspect every occurrence of multiple similar residential deck components;

6. perform any procedure or operation or to enter any area that may, in the opinion of the inspector, be dangerous to the inspector, to other persons, or that may cause damage to the property or to components;

7. move personal property, plants, soil, snow, ice, or debris;

8. dismantle any residential deck component; and

9. determine causes of or reasons for the condition of residential deck components identified in 3.3.B.

13. DEFINITIONS OF ITALICIZED TERMS

Client A person who hires an inspector to perform a residential deck inspection.

Component A primary part of a functionally related group that works together as a system, not including ancillary parts that do not contribute to the intended function of the system.

Cosmetic issues Defects that are superficial, and that do not affect a component's ability to function properly.

Deck construction guideline A written and recognized authoritative reference that describes a recognized and generally accepted deck construction practices; examples include, but are not limited to, The American Wood Council publication Design for Code Acceptance 6 (DCA-6), and The International Residential Code for One and Two-Family Dwellings. Parts of a deck construction guideline that are identified as Appendix, Commentary, or that have similar identifications, are not part of a deck construction guideline. References in a deck construction guideline to other standards, guidelines, and documents are not part of a deck construction guideline; examples include, but are not limited to, the National Design Specification, and ASTM standards.

Further evaluation Additional examination and analysis by a qualified professional.

Home inspection An inspection performed using The ASHI Standard Of Practice For Home Inspections.

Inspect The process of examining readily accessible residential deck components using this Deck Standard.

Inspector A person who has the qualifications to perform a residential deck inspection using this Deck Standard.

Installed A residential deck component that is connected or set in position and prepared for use.

Readily accessible A residential deck component that is located in an area where access will not involve risk to persons or property, and that is visible without: (1) moving matter or material of any kind, and (2) using tools, and (3) using a ladder taller than twelve feet.

Residential deck A wood-framed structure that is located outside of the building. A residential deck may include structures such as a balcony, deck, landing, stairway, and porch. A residential deck may be attached to the building, or it may be free-standing.

Residential deck component A component that is installed and that is part of a residential deck.

Residential deck inspection The inspection by a qualified inspector of residential deck components specified in this Deck Standard.

Technically Exhaustive An investigation that involves the use of advanced techniques, instruments, testing, calculations, engineering, or other means.

Unsafe A condition in a readily accessible, installed residential deck component that is judged by the inspector to be a significant risk of serious bodily injury during normal, day-to-day use; the risk may be due to damage, deterioration, improper installation, or a change in accepted deck construction guidelines.

This American Society of Home Inspectors Auxiliary Standard of Professional Practice for Residential Deck Inspections is the property of The American Society of Home Inspectors, Inc. ©2017, and is used here with permission.

APPENDIX C: DECK EVALUATION CHECKLIST

Defect Num.	Defect Description	Accept. Unaccept. Unsafe End Life Not Insp.	Eval. Action.
2	**Deck Flashing**		
2.1	Absent, improperly installed, damaged, deteriorated deck flashing	A U UN EL NI	E AC
3	**Deck Attachment to Building**		
3.1	Nailed or screwed deck ledger board	A U UN EL NI	E AC
3.2	Deck ledger board attached through wall coverings	A U UN EL NI	E AC
3.3	Improper deck ledger board fastener type or quantity	A U UN EL NI	E AC
3.4	Improper deck ledger board fastener spacing and location	A U UN EL NI	E AC
3.5	Building band joist or rim board does not bear on the foundation	A U UN EL NI	E AC
3.6	Deck ledger board not attached to an approved component	A U UN EL NI	E AC
3.7	Lateral load connectors not installed	A U UN EL NI	E AC
3.8	Deteriorated or damaged wood	A U UN EL NI	E AC
3.9	Deteriorated hardware	A U UN EL NI	E AC

Defect Num.	Defect Description	Accept. Unaccept. Unsafe End Life Not Insp.	Eval. Action.
4	**Guards and Handrails**		
4.1	**Guard post installation defects**		
	No guard posts	A U UN EL NI	E AC
	Posts smaller than 4x4	A U UN EL NI	E AC
	Notched posts of any size	A U UN EL NI	E AC
	Posts spaced more than 6 feet apart	A U UN EL NI	E AC
	Posts secured with only nails or screws	A U UN EL NI	E AC
	Posts attached using bolts smaller than ½ inch diameter	A U UN EL NI	E AC
	Carriage bolts installed instead of machine bolts; fasteners counter-sunk or otherwise damage the post	A U UN EL NI	E AC
	Post bolts do not have washers on head and nut ends, or do not have a nut fully-threaded on the thread end	A U UN EL NI	E AC
	Posts attached to stringer or near other components that cannot resist the twisting loads imposed by the guard	A U UN EL NI	E AC
	Posts attached to deck framing members that are secured using only nails or screws	A U UN EL NI	E AC
4.2	**Guard installation defects**		
	Guard not present at decks and stairs more than 30 inches above a surface below	A U UN EL NI	E AC
	Guard less than 36 inches tall (42 inches where required by local building code)	A U UN EL NI	E AC
	Stair guard with a handrail on top less than 34 inches or more than 38 inches tall	A U UN EL NI	E AC

Defect Num.	Defect Description	Accept. Unaccept. Unsafe End Life Not Insp.	Eval. Action.
4.3	**Guard fill-in component installation defects**		
	Horizontal guard openings allow 4-inch diameter sphere to pass through, including between vertical fill-in components and under any guard bottom rail	A U UN EL NI	E AC
	Stair guard openings allow 4⅜-inch diameter sphere to pass through	A U UN EL NI	E AC
	Triangle formed by riser, tread, and guard bottom rail allows 6-inch diameter sphere to pass through	A U UN EL NI	E AC
	Lattice or other fill-in components do not resist a 50-pound load	A U UN EL NI	E AC
	Wood balusters attached with one nail	A U UN EL NI	E AC
	Loose metal cable fill-in components	A U UN EL NI	E AC
	Insect screens used as guard fill-in components	A U UN EL NI	E AC
	Glazing in guards not safety glazing	A U UN EL NI	E AC
4.4	**Handrail installation defects**		
	Handrail not present at stair with 4 or more risers	A U UN EL NI	E AC
	Unapproved handrail grip dimensions	A U UN EL NI	E AC
	Handrail height < 34 inches or > 38 inches	A U UN EL NI	E AC
	Handrail not continuous from above top riser to above bottom riser	A U UN EL NI	E AC
	Handrail does not begin or end in a post or a return	A U UN EL NI	E AC
4.5	Deck components penetrate wall coverings	A U UN EL NI	E AC

Appendix C Deck Evaluation Checklist

Defect Num.	Defect Description	Accept. Unaccept. Unsafe End Life Not Insp.	Eval. Action.
4.6	**Deteriorated, damaged, loose guards, handrails, and hardware**		
	Deteriorated or damaged wood	A U UN EL NI	E AC
	Red rust on hardware	A U UN EL NI	E AC
	Significant guard or handrail movement	A U UN EL NI	E AC
5	**Stairways and Landings**		
5.1	Improper riser height, tread depth, or nosing depth	A U UN EL NI	E AC
5.2	Improper riser height, tread depth, or nosing depth difference	A U UN EL NI	E AC
5.3	Riser opening between treads allows 4-inch diameter sphere to pass	A U UN EL NI	E AC
5.4	Inadequate stringer support at deck or top of landing	A U UN EL NI	E AC
5.5	Improper drop header installation	A U UN EL NI	E AC
5.6	Improper stringer support at the bottom of the stairway	A U UN EL NI	E AC
5.7	**Stringer installation defects**		
	Stringer not ≥ 2x12	A U UN EL NI	E AC
	Stringer throat < 5 inches deep	A U UN EL NI	E AC
	Cut stringer span > 6 feet, or solid stringer span > 13 feet – 3 inches	A U UN EL NI	E AC
5.8	Improper stringer intermediate support	A U UN EL NI	E AC
5.9	Tread installation defects	A U UN EL NI	E AC
5.10	Landing defects	A U UN EL NI	E AC

Defect Num.	Defect Description	Accept. Unaccept. Unsafe End Life Not Insp.	Eval. Action.
5.11	**Deteriorated and damaged stairways and hardware**		
	Deteriorated or damaged wood	A U UN EL NI	E AC
	Red rust on hardware	A U UN EL NI	E AC
	Significant stringer or tread deflection	A U UN EL NI	E AC
6	**Deck Framing**		
6.1	Floor joists or beams over-spanned	A U UN EL NI	E AC
6.2	Floor joists supported by fasteners, angle bracket, or ledger strip	A U UN EL NI	E AC
6.3	Floor joists or beams excessively notched or bored	A U UN EL NI	E AC
6.4	**Improper joist hanger and connector installation**		
	Inadequate joist hanger vertical load capacity	A U UN EL NI	E AC
	Failure to install fasteners specified by the manufacturer	A U UN EL NI	E AC
	Failure to install a fastener in every round and oblong hole	A U UN EL NI	E AC
	Joist hanger or connector not approved for exterior use	A U UN EL NI	E AC
	Joist in joist hanger seat > 1/8 inch from ledger board or beam	A U UN EL NI	E AC
	Joist hanger flanges splayed	A U UN EL NI	E AC
	Joist hanger damaged, modified, bent	A U UN EL NI	E AC
6.5	Cantilevered floor joists not blocked at beam	A U UN EL NI	E AC

Defect Num.	Defect Description	Accept. Unaccept. Unsafe End Life Not Insp.	Eval. Action.
6.6	Deck beam members not adequately fastened to each other	A U UN EL NI	E AC
6.7	Improper deck beam attachment to deck ledger board	A U UN EL NI	E AC
6.8	Deck beam attached to side of post	A U UN EL NI	E AC
6.9	Deck beam not properly secured to post	A U UN EL NI	E AC
6.10	Deck beam not supported by deck post	A U UN EL NI	E AC
6.11	Splice in multiple-member deck beam not supported by a deck post	A U UN EL NI	E AC
6.12	Deck bracing defects	A U UN EL NI	E AC
6.13	**Deck flooring defects**		
	Flooring over-spanned	A U UN EL NI	E AC
	Failure to install approved fastener type or quantity	A U UN EL NI	E AC
	Failure to leave ⅛ space between floor boards	A U UN EL NI	E AC
	Fasteners installed below the surface of the flooring material	A U UN EL NI	E AC
6.14	**Deteriorated and damaged deck framing and hardware**		
	Deteriorated or damaged wood	A U UN EL NI	E AC
	Red rust on hardware	A U UN EL NI	E AC
7	**Deck Posts and Footings**		
7.1	Deck post too tall	A U UN EL NI	E AC
7.2	Deck post natural defects shakes checks split bow	A U UN EL NI	E AC

Defect Num.	Defect Description	Accept. Unaccept. Unsafe End Life Not Insp.	Eval. Action.
7.3	Deck post not plumb	A U UN EL NI	E AC
7.4	Deck post not in center of footing	A U UN EL NI	E AC
7.5	Deck post not secured at bottom of post	A U UN EL NI	E AC
7.6	Deck footing too small or damaged	A U UN EL NI	E AC
7.7	Deck footing within five feet from building foundation	A U UN EL NI	E AC
7.8	**Deteriorated and damaged deck framing and hardware**		
	Deteriorated or damaged wood	A U UN EL NI	E AC
	Red rust on hardware	A U UN EL NI	E AC
8	**Deck-Related Electrical**		
8.1	No light at deck	A U UN EL NI	E AC
8.2	No GFCI-protected receptacle at deck	A U UN EL NI	E AC
8.3	Inadequate clearance to overhead electrical wires.	A U UN EL NI	E AC

APPENDIX D: DECK FAILURES

DECK FAILURES IN THE NEWS

* = Several Injuries, Exact Number not Reported

ca = Canada

CITY	STATE	MO	YR	INJURED	FATAL
Buffalo Grove	IL	JUN	2001	3	
Emerald Isle	NC	JUL	2001	*	
Ossining	NY	JUN	2001	19	
Parkland	WA	FEB	2001	5	1
Quincy	MA	MAY	2001	5	
San Francisco	CA	NOV	2001	1	
Sea Isle City	NJ	AUG	2001	11	
Egg Harbor	NJ	JUL	2002	4	
Exton	PA	SEP	2002	11	
Point Pleasant	NJ	JUL	2002	33	
St Matthews	KY	JUN	2002	2	
Wildwood	NJ	JUL	2002	10	
Charlottesville	VA	DEC	2003	1	1
Chicago	IL	JUN	2003	57	13
Chilmark	MA	AUG	2003	10	
Chula Vista	AL	JUN	2003	23	
Gauley Bridge	WV	JUL	2003	13	
Huntington	WV	MAY	2003	17	
Queens	NY	AUG	2003	2	1
Tybee Island	GA	JUL	2003	9	1
Chicago	IL	JUN	2004		1
Columbus	OH	NOV	2004	*	1
Elyria	OH	JUN	2004	6	
Highlands	NJ	FEB	2004	7	
Milford	CT	SEP	2004	8	
Pierce County	WA	OCT	2004	7	1
Polson	MT	JUL	2004	80	

Appendix D: Deck Failures

CITY	STATE	MO	YR	INJURED	FATAL
Ross TWP	PA	APR	2004	5	
St Louis	MO	AUG	2004	2	
Tybee Island	GA	MAR	2004	*	
Victoria BC	ca	MAY	2004	10	
Wilmington	NC	OCT	2004	8	
Allentown	PA	JUN	2005	2	
Arlington Heights	IL	AUG	2005	6	
Charlottesville	VA	APR	2005	1	
Chicago	IL	DEC	2005	2	
Durham	NC	MAR	2005	3	
Elm Grove	WI	SEP	2005	9	
Fort Kent	ME	JUL	2005	5	
Lincoln Park	IL	JUN	2005	2	
Loveland	OH	OCT	2005	13	
Minneapolis	MN	SEP	2005	3	
Napa	CA	APR	2001	11	
Portland	OR	AUG	2005	10	
San Francisco	CA	JUN	2005	3	
Seneca	SC	SEP	2005	7	
Sherwood	AR	AUG	2005	12	
Troy	IL	JUL	2005	7	
Virginia Beach	VA	OCT	2005	33	
Annapolis	MD	JAN	2006	5	
Arlington	PA	AUG	2006	3	
Chattanooga	TN	MAY	2006	2	
Chesterfield	VA	JUN	2006	4	
Concord	MA	SEP	2006	6	
Covington	KY	JUL	2006	1	
Fitchburg	MA	JUN	2006	1	
Howells	NY	JUL	2006	15	
Kitchener ON	ca	MAY	2006	2	
Kripplebush	NY	JUN	2006	13	
Lawrenceville	GA	SEP	2006	4	
Marietta	GA	MAY	2006	3	
McGaheysville	VA	JUN	2006	3	
Needham	MA	JUL	2006	2	

Appendix D: Deck Failures

CITY	STATE	MO	YR	INJURED	FATAL
Patterson	NY	JUN	2006	1	
Philadelphia	PA	JUN	2006	7	
Point Pleasant Beach	NJ	JUL	2006	6	
Upper Marlboro	MD	JUN	2006	5	
Westerly	RI	AUG	2006	9	
Brooklyn	MD	MAR	2007	4	
Cape May	NJ	JUL	2007	9	
Fall River	KS	MAY	2007	*	1
Harvey Cedars	NJ	JUL	2007	7	
Melville	NY	JAN	2007	3	
Norman	IL	MAY	2007	6	
Oxford	CT	JUL	2007	4	
Ship Bottom	NJ	JUL	2007	7	
Smithtown	NY	MAR	2007	7	
Vancouver BC	ca	JUL	2007	2	
Warwick	RI	JUN	2007	5	
Wildwood	NJ	SEP	2007	*	
Brentwood	TN	SEP	2008	*	
Chattanooga	TN	FEB	2008	*	
Constantiany	NY	JUL	2008	*	
Houston	TX	JUN	2008	1	2
Narragansett	RI	SEP	2008	*	
Ottawa ON	ca	JUN	2008	6	
Richmond	VA	NOV	2008	21	
Vancouver BC	ca	OCT	2008	3	
Cary	IL	MAY	2009	2	
Lawrenceville	GA	JUN	2009	4	
Ocean Isle Beach	NC	JUL	2009	21	
San Francisco	CA	JUL	2009	1	
Wildwood	MO	JUN	2009	9	
Austin	TX	AUG	2010	23	
Holden Beach	NC	JUN	2010	7	
Kingstowne	VA	JUN	2010	10	
Lexington	VA	MAY	2010	30	
Marietta	GA	JUL	2010	8	
Philadelphia	PA	SEP	2010	7	

Appendix D: Deck Failures

CITY	STATE	MO	YR	INJURED	FATAL
St Louis	MO	MAR	2010	7	
Syracuse	NY	APR	2010	0	
Castleton	VT	SEP	2011	*	
Charlottesville	VA	SEP	2011	2	
Genessee	CO	SEP	2011	2	
Golden	CO	AUG	2011	12	
Jefferson	CO	AUG	2011	4	
Melrose	MA	OCT	2011	0	1
Trappe	PA	SEP	2011	3	
Ashland	NH	MAY	2012	*	
Atlanta	GA	MAY	2012	7	
Austin	TX	JUL	2012	10	
Churubusco	IN	MAY	2012	*	
Forest	VA	MAY	2012	*	
Forest Lake	MN	AUG	2012	4	
Littleton	CO	JUL	2012	4	
Louisville	KY	JUL	2012	4	
Montgomery	AL	DEC	2012	2	
Parkland	WA	FEB	2012	5	1
Powder Springs	GA	SEP	2012	1	
Syracuse	NY	APR	2012	5	
Tallahassee	FL	OCT	2012	*	
Waldport	OR	NOV	2012	4	
Champlin	MN	JUL	2013	4	
Chicago	IL	JUN	2013	1	
Chico	CA	OCT	2013	14	
Concord TWP	DE	SEP	2013	7	
Dartmouth NS	ca	SEP	2013	15	
Gulf Shores	AL	MAR	2013	7	
Long Beach	NY	JUN	2013	5	
McCandless	PA	MAY	2013	*	
Miami	FL	JUN	2013	33	
Montgomery	AL	MAY	2013	*	
New Albany	IN	Dec	2013	22	
Ocean Isle Beach	NC	JUL	2013	21	
Santa Barbara	CA	APR	2013	5	

Appendix D: Deck Failures

CITY	STATE	MO	YR	INJURED	FATAL
Wildwood	IL	MAY	2013	3	
Winona	MN	OCT	2013	8	
Albrightsville	PA	JUL	2014	12	
Atlanta	GA	AUG	2014	5	
Chicago	IL	JUL	2014	1	
Clinton	TN	AUG	2014	1	
Duluth	MN	JUN	2014	0	
Ellenwood	GA	SEP	2014	6	
Folsom	CA	JUL	2014	0	
Greenville	SC	NOV	2014	22	
Halifax NS	ca	SEP	2014	6	
Lithonia	GA		2014	*	
Lynchburg	VA	JAN	2014	1	1
Montvale	NJ	APR	2014	7	
Myrtle Beach	SC	JUL	2014	13	
New Castle	DE	MAY	2014	1	
Oakland	CA	SEP	2014	9	
Pawleys Island	SC	JUN	2014	13	
Penn Forest TWP	PA	JUL	2014	6	
Philadelphia	PA	AUG	2014	1	
Philadelphia	PA	JAN	2014	2	1
Ponte Vedra Beach	FL	JUN	2014	4	
Staten Island	NY	JUN	2014	*	
Stone Harbor	NJ	APR	2014	3	
Stone Mountain	GA	MAY	2014	13	
Towson	MD	SEP	2014	7	
Valley	NE	JUL	2014	2	
Berkeley	CA	JUN	2015	7	6
Beverly	MA	APR	2015	1	
Brome Lake QC	ca	AUG	2015	0	
Burtonsville	MD	AUG	2015	2	
Cedarville	OH	APR	2015	8	
Cole Harbour NS	ca	JUN	2015	1	
Columbia	MD	JUL	2015	5	
Danbury	CT	DEC	2015	2	
Elkton	MD	DEC	2015	4	

Appendix D: Deck Failures

CITY	STATE	MO	YR	INJURED	FATAL
Emerald Isle	NC	AUG	2015	9	
Emerald Isle	NC	JUL	2015	24	
Evans	GA	NOV	2015	0	
Evanston	IL	MAY	2015	*	
Folsom	CA	JUL	2015	0	1
Fort Wayne	IN	APR	2015	2	
Grand Rapids	MI	AUG	2015	1	
Greely	CO	JUL	2015	7	
Hingham	MA	FEB	2015	*	
Knoxville	TN	APR	2015	1	
Lehi	UT	JUL	2015	4	
Lithonia	GA	MAY	2015	9	
New Bedford	MA	JUL	2015	3	
Noblesville	IN	MAY	2015	2	
Northampton	MA	APR	2015	1	
Omaha	NE	JUL	2015	2	
Ottawa ON	ca	JUN	2015	1	
Pittsburgh	PA	JUN	2015	4	
Portland	ME	APR	2015	0	1
Rockland County	NY	JUL	2015	2	
San Francisco	CA	JAN	2015	3	
Sitka	AK	JUN	2015	2	
Yarmouth NS	ca	JUN	2015	12	
Albany	NY	MAY	2016	2	
Alton	IL	SEP	2016	3	
Atlanta	GA	DEC	2016	2	
Atlanta	GA	MAY	2016	4	
Attleboro	RI	JUL	2016	3	
Augusta	GA	JUN	2016	1	
Beaufort	NC	MAY	2016	0	
Bessemer	AL	FEB	2016	6	
Birmingham	AL	SEP	2016	5	
Bridgewater	NJ	JUN	2016	2	
Brooklyn	NY	JUN	2016	16	
Cedarville	OH	APR	2016	8	
Chestnut Ridge	NY	JUL	2016	4	

CITY	STATE	MO	YR	INJURED	FATAL
Chicago	IL	MAY	2016	1	
Clemson	SC	APR	2016	4	
Clifton	NJ	MAR	2016	0	
Colorado Springs	CO	AUG	2016	1	
Corner Brook	CA	JUN	2016	3	
Crownsville	MD	SEP	2016	2	
East Greenbush	NY	MAY	2016	2	
Edgartown	MA	JUL	2016	8	
Erie	PA	JUN	2016	4	
Frostburg	MD	MAR	2016	5	
Gallagher TWP	PA	APR	2016	13	
Halifax NS	ca	SEP	2016	1	
Halifax NS	ca	JUL	2016	6	
Hartford	CT	SEP	2016	31	
Honolulu	HI	OCT	2016	1	1
Lakeside	MT	AUG	2016	11	
Long Beach	NY	AUG	2016	*	
Lowell	MA	JUL	2016	2	
Manchester	NH	NOV	2016	1	
Marathon TWP	MI	MAY	2016	10	
Mechanicsburg	PA	SEP	2016	7	
Medford	OR	SEP	2016	*	
Mill Creek TWP	PA	JUN	2016	4	
Millersville	MD	SEP	2016	2	
New London	CT	SEP	2016	1	
North River NL	ca	JUN	2016	8	
Paducah	KY	JUL	2016	4	
Pennsauken	NJ	JUN	2016	1	
Peoria	IL	JUL	2016	0	1
Philadelphia	PA	FEB	2016	1	
Pikesville	MD	AUG	2016	4	
Pocatello	ID	MAY	2016	2	
Port Vue	PA	JAN	2016	1	
Portland	ME	APR	2016	0	1
Rockville	MD	JUN	2016	2	
Salvo	NC	JUL	2016	3	

Appendix D: Deck Failures

CITY	STATE	MO	YR	INJURED	FATAL
Setauket	NY	AUG	2016	2	
Sikeston	MO	JUN	2016	16	
Sitka	AK	AUG	2016	10	
Soulard	MO	FEB	2016	5	
Suffolk	NY	AUG	2016	2	
Surrey BC	ca	FEB	2016	1	
Topsfield	MA	OCT	2016	1	
Tulsa	OK	JUN	2016	2	
Vero Beach	FL	JUN	2016	*	
Waterloo ON	ca	MAR	2016	2	
Westminster	MA	AUG	2016	1	
Westphal NS	ca	JUL	2016	*	
White Rock BC	ca	JUL	2016	2	
Wonder Lake	IL	JUL	2016	4	
Boca Raton	FL	JUN	2017	15	
Calgary AB	ca	OCT	2017	3	
Cleveland	OH	MAR	2017	1	
Clyman	WI	JUN	2017	2	
Cohasset	MA	JUN	2017	0	
College Park	GA	MAY	2017	5	
Colombus	OH	JUN	2017	2	
Columbia	MO	OCT	2017	0	
Cottage Grove	MN	APR	2017	1	
Cranbrook BC	ca	FEB	2017	1	
DeKalb Co	GA	APR	2017	0	
Destin	FL	MAR	2017	11	
E Hartford	CT	NOV	2017	3	
Edgewater Beach	IL	APR	2017	1	
Gainesville	FL	NOV	2017	2	
Glacier Camp	MT	JUN	2017	50	
Glasgow	KY	SEP	2017	5	
Highland	NY	JUL	2017	10	
Hyde Park	IL	OCT	2017	0	
Kingport	TN	APR	2017	18	
Lake View (Chicago)	IL	MAY	2017	6	
Lehman TWP	PA	APR	2017	12	

CITY	STATE	MO	YR	INJURED	FATAL
Los Angeles	CA	JAN	2017	0	
Manor TWP	PA	AUG	2017	0	
Methuen	MA	SEP	2017	8	
Monona	WI	AUG	2017	2	
Moose	WY	MAR	2017	0	
Oakley SF area	CA	MAY	2017	1	
Perth Amboy	NJ	OCT	2017	1	1
Pleasure Ridge PK	KY	MAY	2017	1	
Port Sheldon TWP	MI	JUN	2017	14	
Roxboro	PA	MAY	2017	11	
San Diego	CA	NOV	2017	23	
Surgoinsville	TN	APR	2017	6	
Virginia Beach	VA	JUN	2017	7	
West Olice	MI	JUN	2017	14	
Wildernest Summit	CO	FEB	2017	0	
Worcester	MA	MAY	2017	9	
Alderrove BC	ca	MAY	2018	2	
Amherst	MA	SEP	2018	0	
Asbury Park	NJ	AUG	2018	5	
Baltimore	MD	JUL	2018	0	
Baton Rouge	LA	AUG	2018	0	
Berkeley	CA	JUL	2018	2	
Binghamton	NY	NOV	2018	2	
Birmingham	AL	DEC	2018	9	
Boston	MA	SEP	2018	4	
Braddock	PA	FEB	2018	1	
Charleston	NY	MAY	2018	7	
Chicago	IL	JUN	2018	3	
Chicago	IL	OCT	2018	4	
Conyers	GA	DEC	2018	6	
Dalewood	MS	JUL	2018	*	
Dayton	OH	JUN	2018	1	
Des Moines	IA	SEP	2018	2	
Ellicott City	MD	SEP	2018	8	
Erie	PA	JAN	2018	0	
Fort Morgan	AL	JUL	2018	3	

Appendix D: Deck Failures

CITY	STATE	MO	YR	INJURED	FATAL
Hartford	CT	JUL	2018	15	
Hartford	CT	AUG	2018	12	
Highland Park	IL	MAY	2018	3	
Johnstown	PA	DEC	2018	3	1
Kansas City	MO	AUG	2018	0	
Little Chute	WI	MAY	2018	1	
Miami Beach	FL	DEC	2018	4	
Monsey	NY	SEP	2018	6	
N Logan	UT	MAR	2018	*	
Narragansett	RI	FEB	2018	*	
Nashville	TN	OCT	2018	0	
Oakland	CA	MAY	2018	3	
O'Fallon	IL	APR	2018	6	
Ottawa	ca	SEP	2018	1	
Pasadena	CA	JUN	2018	10	
Pasadena	MD	JUN	2018	10	
Philadelphia	PA	AUG	2018	2	
Philadelphia	PA	OCT	2018	3	
Philadelphia	PA	SEP	2018	0	
Pikesville	MD	MAR	2018	1	
Pittsburgh	PA	SEP	2018	*	
Rockdale County	GA	DEC	2018	*	
San Francisco	CA	OCT	2018	2	
Savannah	GA	MAR	2018	14	
Sioux Falls	SD	NOV	2018	3	
South Park	CA	MAR	2018	*	
St Louis	MO	NOV	2018	2	
Staten Island	NY	MAY	2018	3	
Stuart	FL	MAY	2018	0	
Virginia Beach	VA	DEC	2018	2	
Whitehall	PA	JUL	2018	10	
Wilder	KY	SEP	2018	0	
Aldergrove BC	ca	APR	2019	40	
Allentown	PA	JUL	2019	0	
Andover	MA	JAN	2019	0	
Arcadia	OH	MAY	2019	*	

Appendix D: Deck Failures

CITY	STATE	MO	YR	INJURED	FATAL
Barron County	MI	JUL	2019	10	
Binghamton	NY	SEP	2019	17	
Birmingham	AL	JUN	2019	2	1
Bridgeport	CT	NOV	2019	5	
Brooklyn	NY	APR	2019	2	
Burlington Ontario	ca	SEP	2019	1	
Calgary Alberta	ca	SEP	2019	0	
Cedar Hill	TX	APR	2019	3	
Chattanooga	TN	MAY	2019	2	
Chicago	IL	JUN	2019	4	
Chicago	IL	MAR	2019	0	
Chicago	IL	AUG	2019	1	
Colona	IL	JUN	2019	13	
Cowansville Quebec	ca	JUL	2019	2	
Cranford	NJ	APR	2019	1	
East Lansing	MI	OCT	2019	5	
Easton	CT	JUL	2019	9	
Fairfield	CT	JUN	2019	6	
Falmouth	MA	AUG	2019	1	
Fargo	NC	Dec	2019	0	
Fire Island	NY	JUN	2019	1	
Forks TWP	PA	JUN	2019	1	
Franklin TWP	PA	APR	2019	1	
Germantown	MD	JUN	2019	100	
Germantown	MD	MAY	2019	3	
Grand Blanc TWP	MI	JUL	2019	0	1
Grand Forks	ND	JUN	2019	5	
Greensboro	NC	JUL	2019	2	
Greenwich	CT	MAY	2019	6	
Hackettstown	NJ	SEP	2019	1	
Haddam	CT	JUN	2019	3	
Indianapolis	IN	AUG	2019	0	
Lakeside BC	ca	SEP	2019	0	
Langley BC	ca	APR	2019	40	
Lebanon	VA	AUG	2019	0	
McMinville	TN	OCT	2019	2	

Appendix D: Deck Failures

CITY	STATE	MO	YR	INJURED	FATAL
Monticello	IN	NOV	2019	*	
Mountain View	CA	SEP	2019	1	
Myrtle Beach	SC	AUG	2019	3	
Nashua	NH	MAY	2019	6	
Ocean Isle Beach	NC	MAY	2019	8	
Ottawa Ontario	ca	FEB	2019	0	
Portsmouth	ME	AUG	2019	0	
Redwood City	CA	SEP	2019	4	
Rochester	NY	JUN	2019	1	
San Francisco	CA	JAN	2019	2	
Sea Isle City	NJ	JUL	2019	*	
Sequm	WA	FEB	2019	1	
Somerset Co	PA	JUL	2019	*	
Spring City	UT	JUN	2019	7	
Summit	NJ	SEP	2019	4	
Valemont BC	ca	AUG	2019	7	
Waves Outer Banks	NC	JAN	2019	3	
West Philly	PA	JUN	2019	2	
West Salem	OR	OCT	2019	0	
Wildwood	NJ	SEP	2019	22	
Winter Park	FL	OCT	2019	1	
Wright City	MO	MAY	2019	*	
Avon	VA	JUN	2020	3	
Beechwood	NJ	MAY	2020	2	
Boston	MA	NOV	2020	1	
Boston	MA	Dec	2020	1	
Chicago	IL	JUN	2020	2	
Chicago	IL	SEP	2020	0	
Columbia	MO	SEP	2020	1	
Detroit	MI	JUN	2020	0	
Exeter TWP	PA	JUL	2020	5	
Gaithersburg	MD	SEP	2020	1	
Macon County	TN	JUL	2020	2	
Monsey	NY	MAY	2020	0	
Mount Kisco	NY	JUL	2020	0	
New Orleans	LA	FEB	2020	2	

Appendix D: Deck Failures

CITY	STATE	MO	YR	INJURED	FATAL
Pasadena	MD	AUG	2020	2	
San Diego	CA	DEC	2020	1	
Saratoga	NY	JUL	2020	11	
Surf City	NC	OCT	2020		1
Syracuse	NY	JUL	2020	9	
Virginia Beach	VA	JUL	2020	5	
Virginia Beach	VA	SEP	2020	7	

The information in this table was compiled by Frank Woeste and Bruce A. Barker. This information is based on deck-related failures that were reported in the media. No representation is made regarding the completeness or accuracy of this information.

APPENDIX E: GLOSSARY

A deck system consists of many components. The following are descriptions of common deck components, and of terms that are used when discussing decks. It is important to note that these terms may be called by different names, depending on regional usage.

Angle bracket: a manufactured metal component that is sometimes used to support a joist (often a rim joist) at a beam or at a deck ledger board. An angle bracket usually consists of two pieces of metal made at a 90° angle, with one piece connected to the joist and the other piece connected to the beam or to the deck ledger board. Angle brackets are no longer allowed as a substitute for a joist hanger. Refer to Chapters 3 and 6 for more information and pictures.

Baluster: a vertical component in a guard that prevents things from passing through a guard and falling off of the deck. Synonyms include picket and fill-in component. Deck balusters are often 2x2 wood. Refer to Chapter 4 for more information.

Band board (joist): see Rim joist (building).

Beam: a structural component that supports joists, and occasionally other beams. Most deck beams are usually located at or near the outside end of the deck opposite to the deck ledger board. Synonyms include girder, although this term is not usually used when referring to a deck beam. Refer to Chapter 6 for more information and pictures.

Blocking: a piece of wood that is installed between deck components to connect or to reinforce the components. Blocking is specified when joists are cantilevered beyond a beam, and may be used when securing a guard post to the deck. Refer to Chapters 4 and 6 for more information.

Bolt (machine): a fastener that is used secure two or more deck components to each other. A machine bolt often has a flat hexagonal-shaped head, but may have a slotted-head to accept a screwdriver. The connection is secured using a nut, often with a washer. Contrast: carriage bolt. Refer to Chapters 3 and 6 for more information and pictures.

Bore: to drill a hole in a deck framing member such as a joist or a beam. Refer to Chapter 6 for more information and pictures.

Bow: a curve in wood measured from a straight line along the length of the wood from one end of the wood to the opposite end. Refer to Chapter 7 for more information.

Brace: a structural component that connects a post to a beam or to another structural component in order to reduce deck movement (racking), which can loosen fasteners and, therefore, contribute to deck failure. Refer to Chapter 6 for more information and pictures.

Cantilever: a structural component, such as a joist or a beam, that projects beyond a supporting structural component, such as the building wall or a post. Refer to Chapters 3 and 6 for more information and pictures.

Carriage bolt: a fastener with a (often) square shoulder under a (usually) rounded head. Carriage bolts are not allowed to be used as deck fasteners, although they frequently are used as such. Contrast: machine bolt. Refer to Chapters 3 and 6 for more information and pictures.

Check: separation of wood fibers across the wood grain. Refer to Chapter 7 for more information.

Connector: a generic term describing manufactured metal components such as angle brackets, knee braces, stringer connectors, lateral load connectors, and tread angles. Refer to Chapters 3, 4, and 5 for more information and pictures.

DCA 6: a publication (free download) that describes deck construction best practices. Refer to Chapter 1 BUILDING CODES VERSUS BEST PRACTICES for more information.

Deck: refer to Chapter 1 for a definition of a deck.

Drop header: a stairway component that is usually attached to a deck rim joist and provides a place to connect stringers to the deck. Refer to Chapter 5 for more information and pictures.

Fastener: a manufactured metal component that connects one deck component to another deck component. Deck fasteners should usually be threaded nails or ring-shank nails, machine bolts, or screws. Refer to Chapter 6 for more information and pictures.

Fill-in component: A component in a guard that prevents things from passing through a guard and falling off of the deck. A fill-in component may be any component that complies with certain requirements. Fill-in components include balusters, metal cables, metal bars, glass, and wood. Refer to Chapter 4 for more information and pictures.

Flashing: waterproof materials, such as galvanized steel, woven plastic fibers, and peel-and-stick materials, that are installed to keep water from entering a building, and to drain water away from areas where it might enter a building. Flashing should be installed at the deck ledger and at doors from the deck into the building. Refer to Chapter 2 for more information and pictures.

Flashing (pan): a type of flashing that is installed under door thresholds and window sills that diverts water away from wood installed under doors and windows. Refer to Chapter 2 for more information and pictures.

Flight of stairs: see stairs (flight of).

Flooring: a component that provides the deck walking surface. Synonyms include decking. Wood is the most common type of deck flooring, but deck flooring can include wood composites and metal. Refer to Chapter 6 for more information and pictures.

Floor joist: see joist.

Footing: a structural component that transfers the deck vertical (gravity) loads from the posts to the soil. Synonyms include footer. A footing usually supports a deck post. Refer to Chapter 7 for more information and pictures.

Galvanization: the process of coating steel with a layer of zinc to slow rusting of the steel. The zinc wears away to protect the steel. When the zinc is gone, the steel rusts. More zinc means that the galvanized hardware will last longer.

Guard: a safety system that prevents things from falling off of the deck. Synonyms include guardrail. Horizontal guards are installed on horizontal surfaces. Stair guards are installed on stairs. A guard may be any structure that complies with certain requirements. A guard may, for example, be a full-height or a partial-height wall. Refer to Chapter 4 for more information and pictures.

Guard post: a guard component that provides the primary structural support for a guard to prevent guard failure when a horizontal (lateral) load is imposed on the guard. Refer to Chapter 4 for more information and pictures.

Grade: at ground level.

Handrail: a stairway safety component that provides users of a stairway with a graspable surface to help them traverse a stairway. Refer to Chapter 4 for more information and pictures.

Hardware: a generic term describing manufactured metal components such as fasteners, joist hangers, hurricane ties (uplift connectors), tension ties, posts bases, and post caps.

Heel: the rear part of a stairway stringer seat cut. Refer to Chapter 5 for more information and pictures.

Hurricane tie: a manufactured metal structural component that connects a joist to another structural component (usually a beam) to restrict uplift of the joist caused by wind. Synonyms include uplift connector. Refer to Chapter 6 for more information and pictures.

International Residential Code (IRC): a model (recommended) building code produced by the International Code Council (ICC). Many building departments in the United States use the IRC as the basis for their local residential building code. Refer to Chapter 1 for more about building codes.

Joist: a structural component that supports the deck flooring and the loads imposed by users of the deck and their belongings. Synonyms include floor joist. See also rim joist (deck). Refer to Chapters 3 and 6 for more information and pictures.

Joist hanger: a manufactured metal component that supports a floor joist and may provide uplift load resistance. Joist hangers are usually installed at the ledger or at the beam. Refer to Chapters 3 and 6 for more information and pictures.

Knee brace: a manufactured metal component that connects a brace to a post, to a beam, or to another structural component. A knee brace is used in place of bolts or screws to connect a brace to a structural component.

Lag screw: a type of fastener that may have a square, hexagonal, or round head, a smooth shank below the head, and a threaded screw shank from the tip to the smooth shank. The term is often used to describe larger diameter screws. Synonyms include lag bolt.

Landing: a stairway component at the beginning and at the end of a flight of stairs. Some stairways have one or more landings between the deck and where the stairway ends. Refer to Chapter 5 for more information and pictures.

Lateral load connector: a manufactured metal component that connects the deck to the building when a deck ledger is used as a structural support for the deck. A lateral load connector helps resist horizontal loads that try to pull the deck away from the building. Synonyms include tension tie. Refer to Chapter 3 for more information and pictures.

Ledger (deck): a structural component that is connected to the building and supports joists at one end of the deck. Synonyms include deck ledger and ledger board. Refer to Chapter 3 for more information and pictures.

Ledger strip: a structural component that supports a floor joist at a deck ledger and at a beam. A ledger strip is usually 2x2 wood that is nailed to the deck ledger or beam. Refer to Chapters 3 and 6 for more information and pictures.

Listed: an approval that is granted to a manufactured product by a qualified approval agency that allows the product to be used without questions from the building code enforcment agency when the product is installed according to manufacturer's instructions.

Load: a force that is applied to the deck structural components. Examples include the weight of people, furniture, or snow, or the force of the wind. Decks must be built to withstand vertical (gravity) loads, horizontal (lateral) loads, and uplift loads.

Machine bolt: see bolt (machine).

Nosing: a stairway component that is an extension of a tread beyond a stairway riser. Refer to Chapter 5 for more information and pictures.

Notch: to cut a piece out of a deck framing member such as a joist or a beam. Refer to Chapter 6 for more information and pictures.

Plumb: vertical.

Plumb cut: the vertical part of a stairway stringer where it connects to a deck, usually at a deck rim joist. The entire plumb cut should bear on the supporting structure, unless a stringer connector is installed according to manufacturer's instructions. Refer to Chapter 5 for more information and pictures.

Post: a structural component that supports a deck beam, and is supported by a footing. Synonyms include column. Deck posts are usually wood, but may be steel or other materials such as concrete blocks. Refer to Chapter 7 for more information and pictures.

Post base: a manufactured metal component that connects a post to a footing. Refer to Chapter 7 for more information and pictures.

Post cap: a manufactured metal component that connects a post to a beam. Refer to Chapter 7 for more information and pictures.

Post (guard): see guard post.

Pressure (preservative)-treated wood: wood into which chemicals have been injected under pressure so that the wood is better able to resist deterioration caused by fungi and insects. The layer of preservative treatement is very thin, and any cut or hole in the wood exposes untreated wood.

Rim joist (deck): a structural component installed at the sides and at the end of the deck joists. Refer to Chapter 6 for more information and pictures.

Rim joist (building): a structural component to which a deck ledger is attached. Synonyms include band joist, rim board, and band board. Band board and rim board are sometimes used to describe the component installed around the perimeter of a building floor system when floor joists such as I-joists and trusses are used. Rim joist and band joist are sometimes used to describe this perimeter component when dimensional lumber floor joists are used. Any of these terms are acceptable regardless of the type of building floor system. Refer to Chapter 3 for more information and pictures.

Return: a safety component at the beginning and at the ending of a handrail. A deck handrail should begin and end with a return, or with a post. Refer to Chapter 4 for more information and pictures.

Riser: a vertical stairway component between two treads, or between a tread and a landing. Refer to Chapter 5 for more information and pictures.

Rust: the deterioration of metal (steel) caused by exposure of metal to moisture. The deterioration that is referred to as white rust indicates that the zinc coating protecting galvanized steel is deteriorating. Red rust indicates that the steel is deteriorating. Refer to Chapter 3 for more information.

Saw kerf: a cut in wood that occurs when the saw blade is run past the point where the cut was supposed to end. Synonyms include saw cut. A saw kerf is most commonly found at notches in joists, and where stringers are cut for treads and risers. Refer to Chapters 5 and 6 for more information and pictures.

Seat cut: the horizontal part of a stairway stringer where it terminates at a landing. Ideally, the entire seat cut should bear on the landing, but it may be acceptable if at least 1½ inches of the seat cut heel bears on the landing. Refer to Chapter 5 for more information and pictures.

Shake: a separation of wood fibers along the grain of the wood. Refer to Chapter 7 for more information and pictures.

Shear: to break or split in a vertical direction across a component such as a fastener.

Sheathing: a component that is installed on the exterior walls of a wood-framed building, and is located between the wall studs and the exterior wall covering (e.g., siding, brick veneer). A deck ledger may be attached through certain types and thicknesses of sheathing.

Span: the horizontal unsupported distance between supports of components such as joists, beams, and stringers.

Split: separation of wood fibers along the grain of the wood that runs through the wood to another surface. Contrast: shake. Refer to Chapter 7 for more information.

Square: a condition in a rectangle when the diagonal lengths between opposite corners are equal.

Stairway: a series of risers and treads that allows someone to go from one elevation to another elevation. Refer to Chapter 5 for more information and pictures.

Stairs (flight of): a flight of stairs is a series of risers and treads that begin and end at a landing. A stairway may have one or more flights of stairs. Refer to Chapter 5 for more information and pictures.

Stringer: a stairway component that supports the stair treads. Treads may be supported by cutting triangle-shaped wedges into a stringer, in which case the stringer is called a cut stringer. Treads may be supported on wood blocks or on tread angles attached to a stringer, in which case the stringer is called a solid stringer. Refer to Chapter 5 for more information and pictures.

Stringer connector: a manufactured metal component that secures a stringer to a supporting component, such as a rim board. Use of stringer connectors is uncommon. Refer to Chapter 5 for more information and pictures.

Tension tie: a manufactured metal component that helps a deck component resist lateral loads. Tension ties are used as lateral load connectors and as deck post connectors. Refer to Chapters 3 and 4 for more information and pictures.

Toe: the front part of a stairway stringer seat cut. Refer to Chapter 5 for more information and pictures.

Throat: the area of a stairway stringer between the bottom edge of the stringer and the cut for the tread, or the tread-cut saw kerf if the saw kerf extends past the tread cut. Refer to Chapter 5 for more information and pictures.

Tread: a horizontal stairway component on which one walks when using a stairway. Synonyms include step. Refer to Chapter 5 for more information and pictures.

Tread angle: a manufactured metal stairway component that is attached to a solid stringer to support a tread. Refer to Chapter 5 for more information and pictures.

Tributary area: the number of square feet of deck area that is supported by a footing or a deck ledger board. Tributary area is used to determine the size of deck footings. Refer to Chapter 7 for more information and pictures.

Unsafe: a condition in a readily accessible, installed system or component that is judged by the inspector to be a significant risk of serious bodily injury during normal, day-to-day use; the risk may be due to damage, deterioration, improper installation, or a change in accepted residential construction practices. Refer to Chapter 1 for more information.

Uplift connector: see Huricane tie.

Wall covering: a non-structural component installed on an exterior wall of a building to protect water and air barriers underneath, and to provide a more pleasing aesthetic. Synonyms include wall cladding. Examples include brick veneer, stucco, and all types of siding.

Water (weather)-resistive barrier: a material that resists penetration of liquid water; usually describes materials such as asphalt-impregnated building paper (e. g., #15 felt), house wraps, certain liquid coatings, and certain wall sheathing products. Refer to Chapter 2 for more information.

APPENDIX F: RESOURCES

Deck Inspection Resources (2020)
by
Frank Woeste, P. E., Professor Emeritus, Virginia Tech

Spring is a great time to inspect your deck to make sure it is safe for continued use by your family and friends. The inspection resources listed herein should be useful for accomplishing a meaningful inspection of an existing deck for occupant safety.

Nailed-Only Deck Ledger Connections

Anatomy of an Inherently Dangerous Deck
by Frank Woeste

https://componentadvertiser.com/Portals/0/EasyDNNnews/Uploads/220/1707%20ATW.pdf

Is Your Deck Safely Connected to Your House?
by Frank Woeste, Loren Ross and Paul Coats. American Wood Council, WoodPost, May 2020

https://www.awc.org/codes-standards/publications/dca6/deck-connection

Repairs needed for more than 150 decks after balcony collapse
by Brooks Jarosz, WSYX/WTTE

https://abc6onyourside.com/on-your-side/6-on-your-side/repairs-needed-for-more-than-150-decks-after-balcony-collapse (14 photos included)

Deck Inspection

Evaluating an Existing Residential Deck
by Frank Woeste

https://componentadvertiser.com/Portals/0/EasyDNNnews/Uploads/207/1708%20ATW.pdf

Deck Codes and Standards (Black + Decker, 2017)
by Bruce Barker

https://www.amazon.com/Black-Decker-Deck-Codes-Standards/dp/1591866855

DCA6 Prescriptive Residential Wood Deck Construction Guide
by the American Wood Council
(This document can be used as a benchmark for safe deck details. Frank Woeste)

https://www.awc.org/pdf/codes-standards/publications/dca/AWC-DCA62015-DeckGuide-1804.pdf

Coastal Deck Issues

Coastal Decks: Red Rust on Decks is a Safety Warning
by Frank Woeste, Joe Loferski, and Bruce Barker. ICC BSJ Weekly, 2019 Sept. 12th

https://www.iccsafe.org/building-safety-journal/bsj-technical/coastal-decks-red-rust-on-decks-is-a-safety-warning

Coastal Decks: Red Rust on Decks is a Safety Warning
by Frank Woeste, Joe Loferski, and Bruce Barker. ASHI Reporter, August, 2019

http://www.ashireporter.org/HomeInspection/Articles/Coastal-Decks-Red-Rust-on-Decks-Is-a-Safety-Warning-/15420

Ledger Strips and the Code
by Frank Woeste and Joe Loferski. Journal of Light Construction, Code's Eye View, November /December, 2020

https://www.jlconline.com/deck-builder/ledger-strips-and-the-code_o?utm_source=newsletter&utm_content=Article&utm_medium=email&utm_campaign=JLC_111520&

Corrosion Information for Connectors and Fasteners with Wood
by Simpson Strong-Tie

https://www.strongtie.com/solutions/corrosion/wood-connectors-fasteners

Safe and Durable Coastal Decks
by Frank Woeste, Coastal Contractor, 2008

http://www.jlconline.com/how-to/exteriors/coastal-resources-safe-and-durable-coastal-decks_o

Appendix F: Resources

Decay of Deck Components

Detecting Early Wood Decay
by Cheryl Anderson, Joe Loferski and Frank Woeste

https://sbio.vt.edu/content/dam/sbio_vt_edu/documents/Decay article.pdf

Design of Decks and Balconies

DCA6 Prescriptive Residential Wood Deck Construction Guide
by the American Wood Council, 2018

https://www.awc.org/pdf/codes-standards/publications/dca/AWC-DCA62015-DeckGuide-1804.pdf

Typical Deck Details
by Fairfax County, Virginia

https://www.fairfaxcounty.gov/landdevelopment/sites/landdevelopment/files/assets/documents/pdf/publications/deck-details.pdf

Deck Ledger Flashing and Stair Solutions
by Mike Guertin, American Wood Council, 2020

https://www.youtube.com/watch?v=aaIVZoMn6uk&feature=youtu.be

AWPA U1-20 Use Category System: User Specification for Treated Wood
(See Table 2-1 Service Conditions for Use Category Designations for selecting and specifying the appropriate pressure-treated lumber and timbers for deck and balcony constructions.)

https://awpa.com/images/standards/U1excerpt.pdf

Balcony Design is a Life Safety Issue

Balcony Design – IBC Changes and Wood Durability Considerations
by Frank Woeste, Virginia Tech and Don Bender, Washington State University
Civil + Structural Engineer, November 2018

https://csengineermag.com/article/balcony-design/

Five people hospitalized after 4th floor apartment balcony collapses in Grand Forks
Valley News Live, June 8, 2019

https://www.valleynewslive.com/content/news/Five-people-hospitalized-after-balcony-collapses-in-Grand-Forks-511010752.html

Condo deck collapses, leaving owners in dilemma
by John Matarese. WCPO Cincinnati, Oct., 2018

https://www.wcpo.com/money/consumer/dont-waste-your-money/condo-deck-collapses-leaving-owners-in-dilemma

About the Author

Frank Woeste, P.E., is Professor Emeritus at Virginia Tech in Blacksburg, VA. He frequently consults with the public, design professionals, contractors and building code officials on various aspects of engineered-wood construction and residential construction, including decks and balconies. E-mail: fwoeste@vt.edu.

OTHER BOOKS BY BRUCE A. BARKER

Black + Decker Codes for Homeowners

Black + Decker Deck Codes & Standards

Commentary on the ASHI Standard of Practice for Home Inspections

Everybody's Building Code

NHIE Mechanical & Content Manual

NHIE Structural & Business Manual

www.ingramcontent.com/pod-product-compliance
Lightning Source LLC
Chambersburg PA
CBHW061211230426
43665CB00032B/2979